A JOURNEY
OF
RICHES

The Wisdom of Authenticity

14 Stories to Awaken the Power of Your True Self

A Journey of Riches – The Wisdom of Authenticity
14 Stories to Awaken the Power of Your True Self

Published by Motion Media International

Editors: Eric Wyman, Yasmin Phillip, Arynne Priest, Pamela and Anne Pen

Cover Design: Motion Media International
Typesetting & Assembly: Motion Media International

Printing: Amazon and Ingram Sparks
Creator: John R. Spender, Primary Author
Title: *A Journey of Riches – The Wisdom of Authenticity*

ISBN Digital: 978-1-925919-96-7
ISBN Print: 978-1-925919-97-4

Subjects: Motivation, Inspiration, Memoir

ACKNOWLEDGMENTS

R eading and writing are gifts that very few give to themselves. It is such a powerful way to reflect and gain closure from the past; reading and writing are therapeutic processes. The experience raises one's self-esteem, confidence, and awareness of self.

I learned this when I collated the first book in the *A Journey of Riches* series, which now includes forty books with over 400 co-authors from over 50 countries. Writing about your personal experiences is difficult, and I honor and respect every author who has collaborated in the series.

For many authors, English is their second language, which is a significant achievement. In creating this anthology of short stories, I have been touched by the generosity, gratitude, and shared energy this experience has given everyone.

The inspiration for *The Wisdom of Authenticity* emerged from a sincere desire to share gentle yet powerful stories that speak directly to the soul, stories that remind us of our inherent worth and the quiet beauty of living true to ourselves.

Each chapter is an authentic whisper from a different author, offering personal insights into the tender, transformative journey of embracing one's truth. These reflections explore the subtle but profound shifts that happen when we listen to our inner voice, meet self-doubt with compassion, and allow our genuine selves to be fully seen and honored.

Acknowledgments

The contributors illuminate many pathways toward authentic self-esteem, through healing, forgiveness, resilience, courage, and grace. From navigating emotional wounds to discovering inner strength, their experiences offer comfort, inspiration, and an invitation to turn inward with honesty and self-respect.

The Wisdom of Authenticity is more than a book; it is a journey into the quiet spaces where self-worth and truth begin to take root. It reminds us that authenticity is not loud or performative, but a steady, grounded presence that grows over time. This book guides you to walk that path, slowly, bravely, and wholeheartedly, honoring the truth of who you are, one tender step at a time.

I want to thank all the authors for entrusting me with their unique memories, encounters, and wisdom. Thank you for sharing and opening the door to your soul so others may learn from your experience. I trust the readers will gain confidence from your successes and wisdom from your failures.

I also want to thank my family. I know you are proud of me, seeing how far I have come from that ten-year-old boy learning to read and write at a basic level. So, big shout-out to Mom, Robert, Dad, and Merril; my brother Adam and his daughter Krystal; my sister Hollie and her partner Brian; my nephew, Charlie, and niece, Heidi; thank you for your support. Also, to my grandparents, Gran and Pop, and Ma and Pa, who now rest in peace. They accepted me just as I am with all my travels and adventures worldwide.

Thanks to the team at Motion Media International. You have done an excellent job editing and collating this book. It was a pleasure working with you on this successful project, and I thank you for your patience in dealing with the changes and adjustments along the way.

Thank you, the reader, for having the courage to examine your life and consider how you can improve your future in a rapidly changing world.

Again, thank you to my co-authors: **Kat Van Note, Cory MacNeil, Kiki Ypsilanti, David Hiscox, Fiona Marie Williams, Jill Sawchuk, Darla Anne, Diane Pierotti, Debbie Sears, Kateřina Fišerová, Jason Bart, Alexis Godinez, Jojo Tonnaer, and Emily Reid.**

With gratitude,
John R. Spender

TABLE OF CONTENTS

Table Of Contents

FOREWORD

T his book was created through a heartfelt invitation to authors from around the world, individuals willing to courageously share their lived experiences and insights into what it truly means to live authentically and honor one's self-worth. *The Wisdom of Authenticity* is a rich blend of voices, each offering an honest and deeply personal exploration of how authenticity and wisdom are discovered, challenged, and strengthened through life's trials and triumphs.

Every contributor brings a unique perspective, illuminating the many ways we can reconnect with our inner truth, reclaim our value, and cultivate a genuine sense of self-respect. Their stories remind us that authenticity is not a destination, nor a linear process, but an evolving journey shaped by vulnerability, reflection, resilience, and courage.

Storytelling has always been humanity's most powerful vehicle for sharing wisdom. Even in a fast-paced, technology-driven world, personal stories offer insights that statistics and theories alone cannot provide. Within these pages, you are invited to pause, reflect, and engage with perspectives that encourage growth, self-compassion, and conscious living.

Anthologies hold a special power in personal development. They allow a single theme to be explored from many angles, honoring the truth that there is no one-size-fits-all path. Here, the shared themes of authenticity, self-honoring, and inner wisdom are woven together through diverse lived experiences. You may begin with any chapter, there is no prescribed order, trusting that the story you need most will find you at the right moment.

Personal growth is a lifelong journey. Just as the universe is continually expanding, so too are we when we remain open, reflective, and willing to explore new ways of being. This book invites you to do exactly that: consider new viewpoints, reflect on your own experiences, and gently cultivate the clarity and confidence to live in alignment with who you truly are.

I hope this collection empowers you to embrace your truth, recognize your inherent value, and walk your path with courage, compassion, and self-respect. As Albert Einstein wisely said, "We cannot solve problems with the same level of thinking that created them." With that in mind, allow your authenticity to guide you, whether you read from beginning to end or open to a chapter that calls to you, and let these stories illuminate your journey toward living authentically.

With gratitude,
John R. Spender

"Authenticity is the daily practice of letting go of who we think we're supposed to be and embracing who we are."

— Brené Brown

The Power of No

By Kiki Ypsilanti

I s it possible for one small word of only two letters to contain so much power, freedom, and most of all, authenticity? How often do we use it? How often should we use it in our lives to be authentic?

Its task is difficult and scary and not everyone who hears it likes it. But the unraveling magic after someone receives it, is you can see this person's true colors, or personality. It's a win-win scenario where both the provider and receiver of "no" reveal their genuine substance and truth, no matter how hard they tried to keep it hidden before.

This word carries lifetimes of wisdom and is one of the biggest tools humans have to fulfill a divine purpose: to find their authenticity.

***

"No," Kiki replied to her parents with a calm, steady, and firm voice for the first time in her life.

How could she do that? This was weird. Even her parents remained speechless for a few seconds until they fully comprehended the extent of their daughter's refusal to meet their needs and expectations for the very first time. They believed they deserved to ask for financial support from their firstborn thirty-year-old daughter, a day after her wedding in a foreign country. Threatening and blackmailing their child was typical behavior for them, as they felt she owed them, after all they had done for her. She was expected to respond with submission, as rejection was never an option; otherwise, she would face the consequences.

Kiki grew up wearing the mask of the good girl. Always obedient, dependable, and ready to meet the needs of others, especially her parents. She shaped her identity around making sure everyone else was happy, even if it meant silencing her desires. She believed that being what others needed her to be would keep her safe, valued, and loved.

This coping strategy became her way of surviving but not truly living. In her quest for approval, she lost touch with her authentic self. People pleasing was not just a habit; it was who she thought she had to be. The wisdom she had yet to discover was that true freedom begins the moment you choose to honor your truth over others' expectations.

When her inner whisper became a scream for help, a cry to finally put herself first and protect her from the constant emotional depletion and abuse of her parents, the result was a simple and powerful "no." The word spread across the universe as its ripple effects started to form.

And that's how it all began....

***

What is authenticity?

"Well, Kiki, it means to be authentic. Isn't it obvious?" a dear reader could reply.

Ok, but what does being authentic really mean? Does it mean to be successful? Does it mean to be happy all the time? Or does it mean to always be the victim of life and righteously complain about everything and everyone?

Authenticity is the ultimate goal and purpose of humanity. It is the journey of unlearning who you are not to find out who you truly are. Deep down, I believe we are all born perfect, pure, true, and authentic. Our upbringing builds layers over our true personality with its bombardment of rules, restrictions, indoctrination, and limitations from family, society, religion, and education. These layers hide our true selves with limiting beliefs, confining our true nature to the darkness of the false persona we present to the world. We put a smile on our faces to fool ourselves into believing we are happy, while inside we cry for help. We think if we work hard enough, we will finally feel enough. We act as if everything is perfect by numbing the pain with addictions, while everything is falling apart.

The pursuit of happiness is a common myth because it is based on illusionary, consumeristic foundations. On the other hand, the pursuit of authenticity is a doable task and a very promising one, as it brings together not just the pure joy and fulfillment of being truly yourself, but also an endless bliss and euphoria. When you are authentic, you can always help others by giving from a full cup and not an empty one.

Ironically, to achieve authenticity, you don't have to achieve anything. From my perspective, you already are authentic. You only have to remember what it feels like by getting rid of all the layers that hide and suppress your true self. The process can be painful and tearful, like peeling an onion, one layer at a time, but it is worth it. My story unfolds as I shed these layers during an ongoing healing journey, an inner work that has finally brought me to where I am now, much closer to my authentic self.

They say everything happens for a reason. I say every event, even a negative one, is a blessing in disguise, as long as you choose it to be.

I had a mental breakdown twenty-four hours after the biggest "no" in my family's history. I received threats and curses from my beloved father, who was always my idol set on a pedestal. A decade of therapy seemed to be my own odyssey, my journey back home. If only I knew then that home meant me. I made a promise that I would never be the same kind of parent to my children as mine were to me. That decision gave me strength to start healing before I gave birth to my first child.

I always felt strange and different, an ashamed outcast, the black sheep, unwanted, unseen, not good enough. These subconscious beliefs were an everyday normality for me. I was anxious all the time, extremely jealous and insecure, and constantly feeling the need to prove myself worthy of attention, support, and love. I was a workaholic and a full-blown perfectionist. I always felt that if the rooms were tidy and clean, the clothes were carefully folded, or if things were in their right place, everything would be under control. The sad truth was I had no control inside myself and I was desperately trying to control the outside circumstances. Anger and frustration could appear at any moment if I felt criticized or exploited, but I felt I had no other choice. I was helpless and it was hopeless.

My inner child had been screaming for what it deserved. For many years, I tried to make others listen when I was the only one who had to. The only people I trusted had emotionally neglected, abused, gaslighted, manipulated, and maltreated me, and I lost myself. I was confused and felt the world was not safe for me. I carried on a mask that had my name on it, but underneath, my true self was hidden.

My body, of course, would follow this emotional dysregulation. Physical symptoms such as irritable bowel syndrome, eczema, and heart palpitations appeared and conquered my physical vessel. Doctors, treatments, and medication would temporarily give relief until the next triggering of my soul. Overwhelming stress would wake my inner demons.

During these first years of my journey to authenticity, I had countless ups and downs, breakdowns and breakthroughs, and now I can see they were all a part of a much bigger picture. Even the boulders were steppingstones and not the obstacles that terrified me then and brought me to my knees. Misfortunes are blessings in disguise, remember?

As I peeled back the layers of blocked emotions and limiting beliefs, I realized I was unraveling pieces of an identity that was never mine. These patterns were not who I was. They were coping mechanisms I had clung to for survival. In the silence between breakdowns and breakthroughs, books found me. They became a lifeline, offering knowledge that awakened something deep within me, a longing to remember who I really was. Beneath the fear, insecurity, and anxiety that shaped little Kiki, I sensed a truth refusing to be buried. I was not who they told me I was. The wisdom of authenticity whispered that I was something far greater, someone whole, grounded, and real.

It took me ten years to find the courage to cut contact with my biological family after my sister's wedding. It was one of the scariest things I ever had to do and, in the beginning, just the thought of it gave me chills of fear and anxiety. Events that took place then made me realize that even though I had already set healthy boundaries with my parents, while I was pregnant with my first daughter, they would never respect them or change their behavior. I could not change them, and that hit me hard. Suddenly, I realized I could only change myself. Relief came after the first shock of explaining my decision to my mother on the phone.

"Anyway, you can never heal in the same environment that made you sick in the first place, Kiki," my tiny inner voice kept reassuring me while my throat became sore from the tears that had not yet come out.

Of course, the reaction and side effects were immense. Fights, constant threats, gaslighting, and emotional manipulation began until I blocked every number they had. Peace finally arrived inside me, and I welcomed it like warm sunshine after a cloudy, rainy day.

My inner work and journey to authenticity skyrocketed after I cut ties with them. I could finally breathe and concentrate on my family's wellbeing, my children's upbringing, my relationship with my husband, and discovering who I really was under the invisible mask.

One evening, several years later, my firstborn daughter became the teacher and I became the student, humbler than I could have ever imagined. Some people believe children should always listen to and do what their parents ask of them. That's their job and that is why they were born. I say exactly the opposite; parents should always have their ears and eyes open to truly listen and watch their children's joy, enthusiasm, curiosity, questioning, and authenticity. Children are our paradigm, and parents should be inspired to mimic them.

My oldest child was just nine and my youngest was five. The three of us were enjoying the pool and the summer breeze during a late afternoon swim. The youngest one complained about something that her sister refused to comply with and immediately, a fight between them started. Instinctively, I rushed into the middle and tried to stop it by doing a very familiar thing; I accused my oldest of being responsible for the argument and attacking her with a look of despise and disgust.

I was comforting my youngest one in my arms and kissing her, while temporarily the noise was paused and then a trembling voice reached my ears saying, "It's fine! If I don't have you, I will always have my dad, at least, and it's fine!"

A thunder must have struck my psyche in those few seconds and my heart broke open into a million pieces. I looked up at her tearful face, full of pain and determination simultaneously.

When my nine-year-old daughter firmly said her own "no," it triggered something deep and painful in me: an old, familiar wound I thought had already healed. In that moment, I saw myself becoming exactly who I had worked so hard not to be—my mother. Without realizing it, I had mirrored the very patterns that once hurt me. My mother always favored my younger sister, leaving me feeling unseen, unworthy, and desperate to earn love through perfection. Now, despite all my inner work, I was unconsciously repeating that cycle with my oldest daughter. It was a heartbreaking reflection, but also a powerful awakening. The wisdom of authenticity revealed itself in having the courage to face these truths, own them, and choose a different path. Healing isn't about never falling; it's about choosing, again and again, to return to who you truly are.

That night was one of the darkest nights of the soul I had. After putting the girls to bed, I ran into my room and cried hard. It was an authentic moment when I could clearly see myself by seeing what I was not. And what I was not, was there in front of me. I was looking the beast in the eyes one last time. I felt all the intensity of the overwhelming sadness and grief and didn't deny it, push it away, distract myself from it, or ignore it. Feeling all emotions is a mandatory step towards our authenticity and, although scary and uncomfortable, it is our birthright to do it. "Feel it to heal it" is a profound quote and it holds so much truth.

That moment changed everything. It cracked something open inside me and allowed my true self to emerge. From that point on, I related to my firstborn not from old patterns, but from a place of authenticity. Our once-turbulent relationship softened, shifted, and found new ground. I finally stepped into the mother I had always longed to be, not because I was trying to become her, but because she had been within me all along. I lifted another heavy layer from my soul, and in its place, a quiet voice rose up, clear and steady, whispering the liberating truth of who I really am. That is the power of authenticity. It doesn't demand perfection, only presence and the courage to be real.

But the wisdom of authenticity would not stop there. In 2017, I experienced the most horrible physical pain I could ever imagine. I suffered from an acute nerve block inflammation, which happened after a muscle cold. The neck stiffness was nothing compared to my right-hand nerve strain, penetrating through the entire length of my hand. It was impossible not to cry from the intensity of the excruciating pain. There was nothing to offer me relief. Even the strongest painkillers weren't effective. The neurosurgeon advised neck surgery if the symptoms wouldn't go away with conventional physiotherapy. Today, I recognize this as another awakening to my true self.

The night before the medical appointment, I decided differently and I experienced an instant recovery by me, to me, for me. I communicated for the first time with the intelligence of the magnificent human body I carry with me. I talked to it and asked how I had mistreated it. And then, I listened. I was overexercising, overworking, malnourished, and dehydrated. I acknowledged and accepted the fact I had not respected it and I made a promise to it – that I would always show it my love and honor it from now on by changing my lifestyle immediately. That night, I forged such a strong connection between my psyche and my body, I felt a warm sensation spreading from my previously painful right hand and down to my numb fingertips, where the nervous torment had finally arrived. In the end, I thanked it as sleep came upon me. The next morning, the pain was totally gone and the feeling of my arm and my hand was back to normal. I have never had that pain again.

Being connected with our body is a sign of genuine authenticity and that awful incident of nervous inflammation was the spark I needed to awaken and reestablish this connection.

Sometimes, though, the universe conspires for us to remember who we truly are and maybe more accidents are required to do that. These accidents are not stop signs. They act as deviations to bring us back to the right path for us.

That's how, in 2018, I had a very simple elbow injury, which developed to a diagnosis of a serious tennis elbow syndrome, that prohibited me from doing my job as a dental surgeon efficiently. I specialize in gum disease treatments and my hands are my tools to earn my living. I suffered for six months with this discomfort, working at the same time, and wearing a special splint, which restricted my hand movements and surgical efficacy.

Physiotherapy, cortisone injections, and massages helped a little, but the pain was still there, as if my body was trying to talk to me… again. And I listened, as promised. What I heard was "yoga." Something was telling me in my gut that I should start learning yoga. I did. And a new chapter in my life's book was beginning, as yoga was the starting point of exploring the depths of my spirituality and the expansion of my consciousness. And, of course, returning to my authentic self. Books, podcasts, online seminars, masterclasses, and lessons were my everyday reality. The tennis elbow was left behind, forgotten and fully treated as if its purpose was done.

Although I was successful in my profession and well-known in my community, I suffered at work. I went to my dental clinic each morning with a heavy heart, feeling suffocated by the overwhelming burden of having to deal with difficult, non-cooperative patients in the dental chair. I really hated the fact that I had to make delicate surgical procedures into such a small field as the human mouth, under local anesthesia, on people who didn't want to help their dental surgeon by actively taking part in their therapy. I dreaded the neck or back pain I had afterwards, because of the adjustments my body would make in order for me to work in the oral cavity. I stopped enjoying what I always loved to do and that was to heal others.

Dentistry was an easy choice for me to make at seventeen, when I was asked to decide my professional future. I wanted to start a family and have children at some point, and by not choosing medicine, which required many more years of education and practice, I could be a mother at an age of my choosing, not my job's. I studied dentistry, and I loved it for a long time. Until I didn't.

It was so easy for me to blame others for what I was experiencing and play small, behind the scenes, as the victim of circumstances and people. Me, poor Kiki. How could I possibly continue this type of working and living? It was out of my reach. I could change nothing on the outside. I felt helpless once more. Sound familiar?

Yoga and its philosophy widened my spectrum of understanding, broadened my horizon of comprehending myself, and removed many false lenses that kept covering my soul's eyes and never let me see beyond the obvious. By learning to be in my body in each pose, I slowly learned to live in the present moment and be in the now. The body, mind, and soul connection brought my presence into life and my beingness back to the light. It was invigorating to meet my real self, one yoga asana at a time.

One question was enough to reframe the victim mentality I had and redirect the energy from them to me, from external blame to inside exploration, not "why," but "what for?" Instead of asking, "Why is this happening to me now?" I asked, "What is the lesson behind the event teaching me about myself?" I finally realized that becoming authentic means taking personal responsibility and facing the totality of self, aiming to love it. Unconditional love doesn't have to be taught to us by our caregivers. It's already inside of us as long as we remember it and reignite it.

These realizations brought me face to face with the raw and transformative wisdom of authenticity, beginning with compassion for myself. When I stopped pretending, performing, and judging myself so harshly, I could finally see others through a clearer, truer lens. It became undeniable; my patients were not trying to frustrate me or make my job harder. That was my filter and unhealed perception projected onto them. In truth, they were struggling with anxiety, phobias, trauma, depression, and emotional pain, often buried beneath the fear in the dental chair. Their behavior wasn't personal. It reflected their suffering. And once I saw that, everything shifted. The wisdom of authenticity taught me that when we stop reacting from our wounds and start responding to our truth, we meet others with understanding and compassion, instead of judgment. I let go of the need to take it all personally, and in that release, I found both freedom and connection.

> *"If we change the way we look at things,*
> *the things we look at change."*
> — *Dr. Wayne Dyer*

After this deeper understanding and being more compassionate and authentic with myself and my patients, I wanted to contribute to their wellbeing in a more holistic manner. How could someone be willing to be treated if their fear of the dentist would not let them function properly under the dental mirror? How could someone preserve the best dental outcome with the proper maintenance care program if procrastination was relentlessly hitting them? The intention was set and it was strong. I wanted to help my patients heal first inside and then outside. I just didn't know how.

They say when the student is ready, the teacher appears. That's what happened when a summer afternoon, after work, I decided out of nowhere to book a discovery call with a representative of a revolutionary healing modality based on hypnosis, which is called Rapid Transformational Therapy™ or RTT. That was the answer I was looking for!

For the next year and a half, I studied hard, trained methodically, and practiced vigorously. The revelations about my authentic nature knocked at my soul's front door, session after session. I was supposed to help my patients using this amazing technique, and I found myself many times in tears of relief and self-healing after practicing on myself first. The wisdom that came with the teachings and lessons became noticeable. Undoubtedly, authenticity is a journey, not a destination.

After twenty years as a gum surgeon, I transitioned into a new, additional role as The Mind Surgeon, a certified RTT Hypnotherapist, helping people heal from the inside out. Through hypnotic regression therapy, I also eliminate invisible mental bacteria that silently sabotage their well-being. With specialized mental tools, I help people overcome the deep-rooted issues that not only affect their ability to maintain a healthy, confident smile but also hold them back from living life to their fullest potential.

Changing smiles was just the beginning. Now it was time to transform lives.

And I was so passionate about it! I still am and this time, my passion and need to help others comes not from the core limiting belief of not being good enough and having to heal others to be accepted, seen, and loved. It comes from a much deeper and profound knowing of myself, a sense of belonging, self-trust, self-love, and meeting the purest version of me. I give now from the overflow of me, not the absence of me, self-honor instead of self-sacrifice. I prioritize my authenticity, and I show others how they can do the same, not with words, but by being a humble living example of it.

Being authentic, for me, is feeling comfortable and open to myself, naked from fake distortions about who I am. It is an act of courage and bravery to be authentic these days. Not everyone can appreciate or accept it. And that's fine, as long as you accept it.

> *"True love is the ultimate self-expression of your authenticity. Offering your truest self to you and others is how you love unconditionally."*
> — *Kiki Ypsilanti*

***

What about my parents? I am glad you asked. Nowadays, I thank them from the bottom of my heart, because finally I can see how they contributed to the wisdom I gained while finding my authenticity and true self. They were a great living paradigm of the universal law "hurt people hurt people," and I can acknowledge that with clarity and genuine compassion. They obliviously gave me the motivation to expand and grow. I transformed the fire meant to burn me into the most powerful fuel. It is a matter of personal choice and each one of us can make that choice.

That's why I love them more than ever now, genuinely and unconditionally. Authentic love is accepting others where they stand in life, as they want to be, and not pushing them to become something they are not willing to, just because you desperately need them to be. Love is accepting the totality of your authenticity first and then the authenticity of others. This is the only way of truly loving the world around you.

I still keep them away for the sake of my inner peace and my children's emotional safety, but as forgiveness shows me its real face, which for me is not to forget, but to go beyond the trauma as my truest self, I find myself more and more attracted to the idea of a final closure by meeting them again one day and just being me. Authentically me. From a higher perspective, they will know they helped through the whole process of me becoming me. They will know they acted as the catalyzers for the wisdom of my authenticity. Mission accomplished.

> *"What you fight, you feed. What you embrace, you release.*
> *And when you release you become authentic."*
> — *Kiki Ypsilanti*

"The authentic self is the soul made visible."

— Sarah Ban Breathnach

Will the Real Me Please Stand Up

By David Hiscox

W hat does being authentic mean in real life? I guess if you asked many people this, you would get a multitude of answers. However, I believe the responses would all probably be along the lines of: "who you really are," "what you see is what you get," "the real deal," and "an honest person," among others.

An "authentic" person is one whose actions match their words—they are genuine. They are a great friend to have, as they are trustworthy. This person is in true alignment with their purpose. They embody what's often said in our Australian vernacular: "You put your money where your mouth is!" This is easy to say, less easy to accomplish in life, but not impossible!

As a seventy-something-year-old male, I have unfortunately had to deal with inauthenticity during my life. So, what I would like to share with you comes from my life experiences growing up and confronting this "demon" of not being "authentic," and how I overcame such a challenge through education and commitment. Does this mean that I have totally overcome the problem in all areas of my life? I can't say, with all honesty, that it no longer rears its ugly head from time to time, but the temptation to not be authentic occurs less and less often.

I would like to start by identifying what the opposite of "authenticity" is. I guess the term "fake" resonates with me the best.

It speaks to me of a superficial, shallow, and flippant approach to things that exhibits a lack of integrity—especially in behavior and living.

To illustrate this point, we only have to consider the popularity and trustworthiness of a used car salesman or a politician. People widely accept that these have been some of the most untrustworthy occupations in our society. The saying is "if you see their lips moving, they're lying." This may sound harsh, but in many situations this has been the case. Hence, the negative reputation. Is this problem just reserved for used car salesmen and politicians? The answer is a resounding no. So, how do we address this problem?

We have two main powerhouses in our bodies: the brain and the heart. Modern science has linked these two "units" as co-existing and communicating. As being totally and inextricably linked or inter-connected. Jesus points this out to his disciples in Luke 6:45 (New International Version): "The good man brings good things out of the good stored up in his heart (mind), and the evil man brings evil things out of the evil stored up in his heart (mind). For out of the overflow of his heart (mind) his mouth speaks."

Being fake to me, then, means that the heart and mind are not in alignment with each other. This imbalance displays itself through stress levels rising in the body, by not doing what you believe to be right, and by living in contradiction with your beliefs and values. Also interwoven with these characteristics is indecision: "part of me wants this, and part of me doesn't." There's disagreement between the heart and mind—conscious and unconscious thought. We have control over our conscious thought to evaluate and respond to situations on a daily basis. Our unconscious mind is a "processor" that just evaluates facts, processing reality without design, deception, and emotion. If we try to live in conflict with these two parts of our minds, we'll have a real challenge. Only by addressing this incongruence can we deal with the fake and begin to live a life of authenticity.

It has been observed that heart transplant patients can experience personality changes, as the heart of the donor is trying to interact with the brain of the recipient. It would be interesting to hypothesize as to why this is the case; however, it doesn't change the fact that there is an extremely close relationship between the mind and the heart.

To illustrate how conflict between the heart and mind can unfold, let me share with you some experiences from early in my own life. As you read on, you will see how the lack of authenticity in my childhood and into adulthood shaped my life in so many ways. Maybe you can identify with some of these illustrations.

I was born in 1951, the third of six children to my parents—part of the "baby boomer" generation. My mother had her first three children within three years, so she had her hands full. We lived on a farm, and my parents (and grandparents) worked hard. When I arrived, housework overwhelmed my mother. She lacked the modern conveniences of today's homemaker, and keeping the house running demanded a lot of physical labor. Thus, I was just another mouth to feed and look after.

It didn't take me long to work out that I had to compete with my older siblings for love, attention, and priority. I was a bright kid and picked up behaviors and ways of getting attention at a very early age—some of them not very positive! So, instead of just being happy being me, I felt that it was my "duty" to make myself heard, noticed, and the most important one. Some might call this a natural instinct to succeed and be the best, but to most, perhaps it's just part of being a child in a growing family. However, looking back, I feel that I was developing tension between who I knew I was as a child (being happy just being a "normal" kid,) and trying to keep up with and excel at everything my older siblings were good at.

What was at play here was the beginnings of behavior to become someone I really wasn't as a child. I had to prove myself worthy of a place in my peer group, my family, and society generally—or that seemed to be the modus operandi at that point. In reality, I wasn't being me. The drive to be accepted and noticed would be the beginning of my fight with "fakery."

My behavior caused many fights among my siblings and a lot of family tension. I was noticed for all the wrong reasons, sometimes with painful consequences. My mother was so frustrated with me that she sent me to start primary school at the ripe old age of four. Even there, I felt the need to be noticed and excel, since I was out of my peer group age-wise. However, because of my voracious drive to be the best, I even frustrated my teacher. When he found out that I was quite intelligent, he promoted me two classes in one year.

With this change, I got a lot of unnecessary attention for all the wrong reasons as well. Bullying and being belittled by fellow students were common occurrences. This continued into high school until I was fifteen, and I left school to work on my parents' farm. I had had enough of the stress and victimization I felt from school and the education system. Opting out was a conscious decision, even though I really wanted to achieve and become a professional person.

Now I had an interesting dilemma on my hands: I had quit school to work on the farm, a lifestyle I loved. However, I had another "love" I wanted to pursue flying in the Air Force. But I would need to pursue further education and achieve high qualifications for that to happen. Because of the way I had constructed my behavior and life up to this point, I had made a decision wholly with my brain and not my heart. I chose farming, as the other option seemed too hard to handle. I had decided to override my intuition and unconscious mind.

Unfortunately, looking back, this choice only underlined my direction toward not being authentic as a person; in my heart I wanted to be an aviator. This choice would plague me for many years to come.

Enter the late 1960s. A time of change, the "hippie era"—free love, sex, and peaceful existence. We had been born after World War II, and our generation didn't want to duplicate the experience of horror, destruction, and the tragedy of lost lives that our parents had gone through. Life was good until our Australian government decided that they needed to help the United States of America by getting involved with the Vietnam War, a war that only made the suppliers of arms and war machinery rich. And because the fighting was largely guerrilla warfare, which was a new type of war, the battle became unwinnable. So the government introduced conscription to obtain the best from the late teenage population. There were many demonstrations about this, but the government ignored the young peoples 'voices and initiated the call-up.

Fortunately, they didn't conscript me, although I spent many stressful days waiting to see whether my birthdate would be picked in the ballot. Some friends of mine were conscripted, and after those who lived through the war came home, they were indelibly altered in personality by the experience. I never talked with them about it for two reasons: 1) they were quite traumatized by what they had experienced and done; and 2), I felt guilty that they had to experience it and I didn't. So, I felt partly guilty, partly happy that I had "escaped" what they went through. It never sat well with me either way, but just added to the feeling that I really didn't know who I was.

All I knew was that I needed to "find myself," as was the hackneyed phrase bandied about by the hippie teens and twenty-somethings of that era. I knew I wasn't being the real me, but I couldn't find the avenues by which this situation could be resolved. Many of my peers who experienced similar upbringings to me, resorted to alternate methods (drugs, communes, and just generally dropping out of society) to cope with this incongruity of mind and heart.

The repercussions of the Vietnam War affected both those who fought and came back home, and the ones left behind who had to deal with the "fallout" of the returned servicemen. The futility of war and its effects on humanity became painfully obvious to us all. Even today, people my age do not want to relive that era.

This chapter in my life growing up, added to the confusion of who I thought I was (mind), and who, deep down, I thought I knew I was (heart). Up to this point, I had generated some very fixed values and beliefs, molded by my upbringing and life experience. The duplicity of social norms and my beliefs created turmoil in my mind, with more questions than answers. When we don't live in alignment with our true selves, we settle for lives of conflict and disaster. Little did I know that my next twenty or so years would turn basically into a train wreck of an existence.

Looking back on my life now, I can see that so many choices and decisions I made contradicted what was in my heart. I did not understand the heart in relation to my mind, so not listening to my unconscious mind (which I believe resides in our heart mostly), and being headstrong and stubborn, became a recipe for disaster. Being an authentic person was the furthest goal from my mind!

I left the farm for a year to do accountancy (handy for bookwork on the farm), met a girl who stole my heart, had the relationship fail, then fell out with the farm existence and left to pursue another career. I got married on a rebound, returned to farming for a while, then watched my marriage fail after thirteen years. I was pretty upset at the way my life was unfolding. The only good part on the horizon was meeting another lady whom I married, we have been together for over thirty-one years now.

So, you can see that, when we have incongruencies in our life, success becomes an uphill battle. Each year brought its challenges, and I had at least another two occupational changes that presented emotional, financial, and personal challenges. After so many years of internal stress and fighting, I reached the bottom of the barrel around 2008.

Depression had always been lurking on the sidelines, and it made its presence felt during that year. I knew I had a mental challenge that needed to be addressed, but there seemed to be no way I could get any traction in understanding what was unfolding in my mind. And this is the situation with nearly all people who live in a state of internal conflict wondering who they are and how to run their life in harmony with themselves. We could extrapolate here the theory that this incongruency could be a factor as to why suicides are becoming more prevalent. In my case, I believe it was.

As good luck (or Providence, I believe) would have it, I happened to be in Melbourne around the middle of 2008. The weekend my wife and I were there, we heard about a personal development event that was being held. It covered how to break the bonds that bind us to a life of futility and frustration, and how to design a new "self" for ourselves. Out of curiosity, we both went, and the result was profound. Over that weekend I gained a new understanding as to why my life had been what it was, how the future didn't have to be the same as the past, and that I could live in harmony with myself and everyone else. I also learned how our mind works and how to control the different aspects of its operation.

Long story short, I pursued as much information and knowledge as my mind could contain for the next two or three years. I became proficient in mind transformation and change. I now could help myself and others who were struggling with the problem of authenticity. The tools I obtained through study and application gave me new confidence to be myself and be true to my own beliefs and values. I learned to trust my intuition and follow my heart more. Some changes were almost instant, while others were a process. It was a bit like learning to walk again.

I attempted to help my kids in their growth as developing adult humans. I was rudely awakened by the faulty role model they had been exposed to for quite a long time. I had some serious work to do. Most of my kids developed lives that were genuine and stable; however, one had many challenges similar to that of his dad and was a crazy, mixed-up lad.

Armed with the new knowledge I had obtained, along with life experience, I faced the task of helping my son through a frustrating and dark period in his life. It took a lot of open-ended love and personal involvement over quite a few years to help him see how to operate his life in alignment with who he really was, but the journey was worth it.

Establishing mutual trust and helping my son understand through word and example, how to live his life, has been very rewarding. Seeing him just be honest with himself and living according to his beliefs and values has been a wonderful milestone. He and I now have a special relationship, and he has turned out to be stable, happy, and authentically himself. A greater reward would be hard to find.

The commitment to authenticity is one I keep with all my children, who have all grown up and now have children of their own. They now know that they can trust their dad to be what he says he is, and they can trust my advice to them when given.

Another recent experience of providing guidance was when a company I worked for before retirement asked me to train a young lad to do my job. This was requested so my position would transition to him seamlessly. Now, Tom (not his real name to protect his identity) came from a very dysfunctional family. His parents were well-meaning, conservative, and religious people, but his mum was a control freak over her children, especially Tom. He was the baby of the family, so she wanted him to grow up with her beliefs and values into adulthood.

Tom came to me for training when he was twenty-seven years old. He was in a relationship with a girl he loved. His mother didn't approve because the girl was not living according to the family's conservative religious beliefs, and subsequently, drove a confusing wedge between Tom and his girl, whom he loved and wanted to spend the rest of his life with. His mother demanded she rubber stamp her approval on any decisions he made in his life up to this point.

Not only did I have to train Tom to do my job, but I had to help him understand that he wasn't living authentically at all in this situation. Over the span of the next six to twelve months, we were able to work through his inability to follow his intuition and be true to himself. He had to stand up to his mother to operate his life according to his values and beliefs, and start a new life and relationship with his girl, which he did. He now has a great relationship with his partner and has a little daughter of his own. His mother has fortunately bowed out of needing to control his life and has left him to live according to his own beliefs and values. Tom has matured into a responsible employee, adult human, and loving dad.

I remember one of the last times we had a discussion before I retired from work. He told me, "Dave, I want to thank you for what you have done for me over the last year. Not only have you imparted your work life experience to me, which is invaluable, you have shown me how to be a good and genuine person." There is nothing more rewarding than this. All of this would not have been possible if I hadn't changed my life from one of "fake it till you make it" or had not been willing to change into a state of authenticity.

If you feel your life may be one of "fakery," and you are not being true to yourself and what you believe you should be, then what steps can you take to do something about this?

Establish what beliefs about yourself are important and what major values you have that govern how you live and operate your life. Are these values important enough that they are "non-negotiable"? If not, why not, and what are you going to do about them? If you don't stand for something, you'll fall for anything!

Here are a few other important questions you should ask yourself in order to successfully adopt a life of authenticity:

- Is my life running in line with my beliefs and values? Is my word my bond? How do others perceive me when I look introspectively?
- Am I willing to confront the incongruencies that make me appear "fake" to others, and have I the courage to take on this important change and challenge? What would this mean to me, and to others with whom I associate?

To live a life of authenticity, these questions need answering. If you have difficulty confronting the answers to these questions, seek help from someone trained in these areas—doing so will pay enormous dividends in your life and future!

Now, it would be misleading if I said that my life has been a "bed of roses" since the point when I decided to live authentically. What we put into existence in earlier times still has repercussions now. I am still a fallible human whose past occasionally pops up to haunt me. However I have the tools to deal with these situations, and they are not insurmountable challenges anymore. Now I trust my intuition and operate with it, as it is my heart telling me the right way based on my values and beliefs. I am not afraid to speak my mind when it is demanded of me, and I do it with truthfulness and integrity. Gone are the days when social pressure and opinion caused me not to have an opinion and not be able to express it.

It is a new experience to learn to give your heart and mind an opportunity to listen to each other, not one stifling the other, so that you portray a united personality to the world. What you see is what you get. A portrait of authenticity. "This is who I am."

I wish you all the best in your journey to become fully authentic!

"Authenticity starts with being honest with yourself about what you really think and feel."

— Unknown

Being Myself Was Always Simpler
What I Saw When I Stopped Trying

———————— ⫯⟋⟍⫯ ————————

By Kateřina Fišerová

D *ear friends,*
There is nothing I love more in this world than writing
letters. I write them often—to friends, to clients, to life itself, and
sometimes even to myself. This format allows me to open up fully
and share what flows from my heart or, as we say in Czech, "what I
have on my heart."

With you, I want to be completely honest and authentic, which is
why I chose this format for my chapter. With humility and love, I
would like to share a part of my life story with you, as truthfully as I
can.

I am an ordinary woman who loves her life. And I feel that life loves
me back. Even if my story may seem exceptional, it is simply one of
many stories unfolding every day.

Thank you for allowing me to share this story, the story of the
Wisdom of Authenticity—with you.

The Feeling That Mattered More Than the CV

When I was looking for my first job after school, I had a clear idea
of what I wanted to do. I liked what I saw in soap operas: girls

walking around the office carrying folders, making coffee, always wearing beautiful clothes. So, I decided to look for a job as an assistant in a marketing department.

I came across a listing for an assistant to VIP clients at an online marketing agency.

Except… I didn't know a thing about marketing. And if I knew nothing about marketing, I knew even less about online marketing. But I believed I could learn.

The night before my interview, I spent hours studying marketing definitions and researching the company. In a magazine, I found a line saying the owner was an untrustworthy miser and that people should be careful with him. You might think that discouraged me. On the contrary, I became curious to meet him and find out for myself.

I believed it would be socially expected to pretend I had experience. But I was so excited about what I had learned in one night that I confessed everything.

And because I was being honest, I even asked whether they could improve the search results for the owner's name so it wouldn't say he was stingy and untrustworthy. I quickly added that he didn't seem that way to me… and everyone laughed. They appreciated my authenticity, and the whole room relaxed.

By the end of the day, they chose an older candidate with five years of experience. I was disappointed but accepted it.

Two days later, they called me back.

The candidate had declined the offer and although they had other experienced applicants, they decided to trust their instincts and follow the wisdom of authenticity.

They hired me.

I Don't Have to Leave to be Happy

Working at the agency was fantastic. I learned so much and became known as the Queen of the Inbox. I had great clients, colleagues, and a boss. But a recurring thought followed me: if you're good at what you do, you should work for yourself.

Leaving was difficult. I didn't know how. A friend suggested I hire a coach. She said coaches could help you do the things you want but can't push yourself to do.

I was lucky to work with Vladimír, one of the first transformative coaches in the Czech Republic. During our very first session, I asked, "How do I start my own business?"

And I left with an entirely different answer:

"I don't have to leave or start a business to be happy."

I realized I had been trying to prove my worth, trying to earn the feeling of being "successful enough." I thought happiness would come afterward.

But I had been happy all along.

Authenticity had been quietly guiding me home.

From that moment, I saw the same pattern in others. When we are unhappy, we chase something we think will give us happiness, instead of going directly toward happiness itself.

Happy people allow themselves to want anything because they know their happiness doesn't depend on it.

When I saw that I didn't have to leave, the pressure lifted. My mind quieted. And from that clarity came a gentle knowing: I actually wanted to start my own business. There was no push, only lightness and playfulness—the natural result of a quiet mind.

I invited my boss to lunch. I worried about what to say. When we sat down, I heard a quiet inner voice: "Tell him the truth."

So I did: "You know, I really like you. I love this job. I love our clients. I have amazing colleagues. I don't want to leave you in the lurch. I'm confused… but I really, really want to try working for myself."

To my surprise, he helped me work out how to do it.

I became a freelancer, and the agency became one of my first clients. Within six months, I helped recruit and train my replacement. Over the next four years, our collaboration continued to grow, built on trust and authenticity.

When I Began to Trust Myself and Life

I used to think that working for myself would be hard. I also believed there were only a handful of clients whose brands would be true "love brands" for me—real passion projects. The truth is, in the early years, there were months when I didn't have money for rent or food, but I never saw it as a problem or as "hard." It simply was what it was. I would pay one bill and move on to the next.

It never felt like running a business was difficult. Sometimes I even felt a little guilty that clients were so eager to work with me and that new ones kept showing up.

By my third year, I was managing more than 40 clients— surprisingly, all heart-centered brands. I had to admit that I could no longer support them all as deeply as I wished. When I realized I didn't have the capacity to help them grow the way I wanted to, I began looking for someone who could take better care of them than I could. I even started arranging meetings for my clients with my own competitors.

My clients weren't eager to leave, and they were surprised I wasn't bothered by the idea of competition. But I wasn't.

Now I see that it was the wisdom of authenticity guiding me. I genuinely enjoyed connecting people who could support and help one another. And I knew that, for some of my clients, my colleagues were simply a better fit than I was.

Throughout those four years as a freelancer, most of my clients used an email marketing platform called SmartEmailing. The support team there knew me very well. We were in touch almost daily, and during quieter times, at least once a week, discussing a client or a feature. I often asked for advice, and gradually I began suggesting improvements and new features. I never criticized them; I simply shared ideas for functionalities that would make my clients' work easier.

One day, I went to visit my mom. She wasn't home yet, so I made myself a cup of tea and sat on the steps outside her house, soaking in the wild beauty of her garden. Suddenly, my phone pinged with a message: "Katka, would you like to lead SmartEmailing?" wrote the owner of the company.

I smiled. Maybe he sent the message to the wrong number? So I replied in my own way: "I'm not sure what that means — let's talk about it. :)"

Within a month, I joined SmartEmailing as the new "boss." I had no experience managing people, let alone running a company... but something in me knew I could trust being true to myself. Authenticity was all I had.

> *"I've never done that before, so I'm sure I'll manage!"*
> *— Pippi Longstocking, Astrid Lindgren*

The Company of My Heart

The owner introduced me to the team at an all-company gathering. That's when I discovered that the entire company worked remotely, with people based all over the country. I remember thinking, *What a great opportunity to finally explore the beauty of my homeland. I'll have a reason to travel!*

When I stood in front of my new colleagues for the first time, I felt shy and a little nervous. The only thought running through my mind was, *Well, here I am. This is me.*

Part of the team was genuinely excited, especially customer support. They finally saw my face after knowing only my emails and my voice. They greeted me with a wave of hugs, and it moved me deeply. It was the warmest welcome I had ever experienced.

But not everyone shared that enthusiasm—especially the developers. They didn't like the idea that someone from the outside, with no prior knowledge of the company, would be leading it. And a woman, no less. I remember that whenever I entered the meeting room, the guys would fall silent.

I didn't want to push anyone or myself, so I began where things felt natural. Guided by the wisdom of authenticity, I spent my first month with each team member, one full day at a time. I asked about their work, their ideas for improving the company, and how I could support them. I listened openly and honestly, wanting to understand them as they truly were. I even tried a bit of everything myself—making collection calls, helping in support, exploring our marketing, and, of course, saving development for last.

Before our one-on-one meetings with the programmers even began, they slowly started to relax around me. Once, instead of a formal meeting, I went out with one of them for a cheeseburger and couldn't get the cheese out of my hair. It broke the ice. When he accepted me, the rest did too.

It was spring, and the team had agreed to host our regular gatherings at someone's home each time. This time it was Martin's turn, our lead developer and the architect of the app. He lived in a family house with his grandfather. I remember that day like it was yesterday—meeting his granddad on the stairs and chatting for half an hour. He told me about his tomatoes and cucumbers, brought me homemade meatloaf, and we exchanged recipes.

I had never seen such large, crystal-clear blue eyes. It felt as if he were pulling me into the very core of his soul. As if I were standing in front of a perfectly open human being. His eyes held so much light and love.

I couldn't wait to find Martin and tell him about my meeting with his grandfather. When I finally did, I began describing those big blue eyes—and then I looked into his.

For the first time in our two years of working together, I saw it.

This man who had once seemed so closed off and distant had the same open, welcoming, and loving eyes as his granddad.

We started talking more and going on trips together. We became close friends. Then we fell in love. We started dating. I moved in with him. Our personal and professional lives became beautifully intertwined.

Around that time, I realized there is no such thing as "time for myself," "time for family," or "time for work." It is all my time—artificially divided into imaginary compartments. This is my life, my time. And no matter what I'm doing or who I'm with, it is still my time. The time of my life.

Authenticity taught me that how I choose to live and savor each moment truly matters. Even then, I knew I wanted to enjoy life fully, in everything.

He Wants to Sell My Company!

We went to visit David, the owner of the company we worked for. We were sitting in his backyard around a campfire, roasting sausages over the flames. The wood crackled beautifully. I still remember the atmosphere of that evening—ease, acceptance, openness, and simply being together.

David looked at me. I could feel how sincere he was, and I sensed he was a little afraid to say what came next.

"Katka, I need to increase the company's profitability. I need you to prepare it for sale. It doesn't have to be right away, but I feel this is what I want."

I saw the shock in Martin's eyes, and I understood.

David wants to sell our company.

Imagine this: you live and breathe something 24/7. It feels like yours. And then someone reminds you that it isn't. It's his. And he can do whatever he wants with it.

We let the conversation sink in. On our way home, stuck in traffic on the highway, it suddenly hit me.

This company is ours. It started as a feeling. It will become a reality. If someone is going to buy it, it will be us.

How We Bought the Company We Worked For — With No Money

I felt responsible for the team, the clients, and our partners. We invited the team leads, key people, and long-standing members of the company to lunch. I wanted to be fully transparent with them—authentic in sharing the truth—that Martin and I might no longer be part of the company. We wanted to buy it, and if not, we wouldn't stay. Honesty and authenticity guided the way we showed up.

One by one, they all said the same thing: if we weren't staying, neither would they. One by one, they told me they would gladly go plant trees with me somewhere, start a nonprofit, do anything at all, even outside of this industry.

Friends, you have no idea how relieved I was. I could finally lay down the weight of responsibility and step back into the game. They were ready for the unknown. And they wanted this company to be ours.

So we texted David: "David, how much do you want for SmartEmailing?"

His reply came instantly: "I've always wanted $5 million. Let's talk."

I didn't have a single penny saved. But I was clear on one thing: it doesn't matter whether you're short $5 or $50 million. The path will vary, but in every case, you must let go of what you know and begin taking new steps—one idea, one step at a time—authentically responding to what shows up.

I didn't know where to get the money, but I had one thing: an inner sense of knowing—the Wisdom of Authenticity. So I kept focusing on what felt clear. Five million didn't feel right. At the same time, I was committed to making sure David received a price that felt good and fair to him. This deal had to feel right for everyone.

I always communicated authentically from the heart. I didn't want to threaten David with leaving the company. That would have made no sense. We weren't two sides trying to win. We were one team facing a shared challenge: a change of ownership.

Through gradual negotiation, I managed to significantly lower the price. We accounted for company-owned assets still in David's use and agreed that if we put $500,000 on the table within three months, the deal would be closed and we'd have four more years to pay the rest from company revenue. Now I didn't need to find $5 million, just $500,000.

I spoke to banks. They wanted massive amounts of data and ten-year forecasts. The truth was, our company's numbers were… punk. We didn't have the reports they wanted. Putting everything together made us realize how amazing SmartEmailing really was. It was more than numbers, more than a business; it was family.

So I reached out to investors I had heard of through the media. I listened to podcasts about startups and investors. I spoke with brilliant financial advisors. But just like the investors, they wanted equity. Some even wanted majority ownership. That wasn't authentic to our vision, and it wasn't what we wanted. Staying true to ourselves mattered more than following the usual path.

When I was preparing the company presentation for potential investors, I decided to add references from key institutions. I sent only three emails: one to a major bank, another to the leading Czech anti-spam organization, and the last to the biggest free email provider in the country, which received millions of emails from us every day.

Two replied immediately, saying they would be happy to become silent investors. Neither asked for hard data. They knew me. That was enough. I wept with gratitude.

What followed was a series of meetings. In the end, we didn't become business partners, but friends. They helped me sort out my thoughts and gain a clearer sense of the possibilities. They supported us then, and they still support us today.

We raised one-third of the amount we needed.

What if the team co-owned the company with us? Or at least the people who gave me courage during that pivotal lunch? The idea filled me with joy. Yes!

In the end, there were seven of us—seven brave souls who pooled together another third of the money for the first installment.

We were still missing the final third. We had one month left. I felt a deep pull to stop thinking about money altogether for a few days. I knew it was the best thing I could do for all of us.

When we feel tangled, the wisest thing we can do is step back from the mind for a while and surrender fully to our own authenticity.

The Final Weeks

My friend Jana, who had been diagnosed with cancer, hadn't reached out in a month. So, I wrote to her husband. Pavel was in a wheelchair, and Jana had been taking care of him for the past few years. He replied that Jana wasn't doing well. I knew SmartEmailing would take care of itself. I wanted to be with Jana.

At first, I stayed with them for just a few days, but in the end, Karolína, (Kája) our mutual friend and I spent Jana's last weeks together. Guided by authenticity, we simply showed up for her: caring, singing, reading stories, and being fully present in each moment, exactly as we were. Some evenings, Kája and I would crawl into Jana's bed and sing folk songs together. Later, when Jana could no longer sing, we sang for her. Sometimes we read her stories.

I'll never forget the fullness of life that filled every moment in their home. Moment by moment, we responded to whatever was right in front of us, guided by our own wisdom of authenticity.

I'll never forget that morning. I took over for Kája in the room with Jana. She kept pulling off her oxygen mask, and I kept putting it back on. During one movement, I heard the bone crack. As she tried to lift herself, her femur had fractured. The pain must have been unimaginable; she moaned softly.

When the doctor arrived to give her another injection for the pain, she slowly began to calm down and breathe more evenly. He took us aside and told us she didn't have much time left. I couldn't understand what he meant. This was how we had been living for weeks. What did he mean, "not much time left?" I felt angry at him.

I returned to Jana's bedside. Her breathing was shallow but steady. Still, I had the strange feeling that she was no longer fully there.

Kája and I stayed by her side. Pavel joined us. The sun was rising. I'm not sure if anyone else was there. We held Jana's hands and watched her chest rise. Inhale. Exhale.

With every breath, it became less certain whether there would be another.

And then she was gone.

It felt as if her body kept going for a little while longer.

Those final weeks of her life, and the moments she allowed me to share are something I will never, ever forget. The wisdom of authenticity brings the understanding that real peace comes not from control but from truth. It is living and dying with openness, honesty, and deep acceptance.

Jana's final days, filled with surrender, laughter, and love, embody that wisdom.

A few days after Jana passed away, after I had returned home, I received a message from Pavel: "Kačí, I heard you need money. I pulled out some investments from abroad for Jana. Let me know how much you need."

I was grateful to borrow the remaining money from Pavel.

The Better Listening World

We bought the company. At the team's request, I stayed on as part of its leadership. Four years later, the company was fully paid off, and every shareholder had received back their initial investment. I felt like I was done.

I haven't mentioned this yet, but for the last thirteen years I had been immersed in exploring the Three Principles and transformational coaching. I fell under the spell of deep listening. I trained with Michael Neill at his Supercoach Academy and later in the Advanced Supercoach program. In the Czech Republic, I founded the project Czechia Listens, and together with the nonprofit Understanding Mind, we run our own coaching school. I'm also part of the Happy Czechia foundation and a board member of the 3PGC.

It felt increasingly authentic to help people fall in love with life, rather than teaching them how to send bulk emails. But I couldn't make the leap. I kept preparing the team for my departure, by slowly stepping back, finding someone to take over my role in the company, yet I was still fully in it. I couldn't leave. So I began taking on more and more meaningful work alongside running the company. I started building A Better Listening World in my own way. I envisioned an international summit that could mark the beginning of a greater change. That was my dream.

Then one day, Martin returned from a photography expedition. He looked exhausted. He said he needed to talk. We sat down in the kitchen, his head in his hands. He lifted it just for a moment.

"Kačenka, this can't go on. I can't do it anymore. We're not happy together."

It hit me like a wave.

And then we both cried and spent the whole day curled up in bed, listening to each other as if we never had before. We said so much to each other. It was raw, authentic, and incredibly deep. I knew he was right. It hurt, and at the same time, I felt immense gratitude that he had the courage to say it. I had been thinking the same thing for years—that he was my best friend, but that we didn't work as a couple… and yet I never would have left him.

You know what felt like a miracle?

The next morning, I woke up and knew I was free from SmartEmailing. I had never had that thought before. But that morning, it was crystal clear. I had stayed in leadership to protect him, to steer the company so the application would evolve the way he wanted it to. I had been his voice. I didn't have to be anymore. And I felt free again.

Isn't it amazing how we can change our minds? Or rather, isn't it wonderful that we can suddenly, overnight, let go of something we've been holding onto for so long?

I dove headfirst into organizing the summit. Martin continued supporting me, and so did everyone on the team. I didn't know what The Listening World Summit in Prague would bring, or what it might spark.

I just knew there was a version of this summit that wanted to happen. And that was the one I would follow. Guided by authenticity, we welcomed about 350 people in person at the Prague Congress Centre. More than 2,700 people joined us online.

My friends,

I don't know where life will take me next. And so I continue, day by day, minute by minute. I sing the song of my heart as best as I can sometimes softly, sometimes out loud following the notes that arise in my soul.

Because when we allow ourselves to be who we truly are, just as we are in this very moment, we realize that everything we need is already within us.

As I rewrote my story to share it with you, a new understanding revealed itself between the lines: within our authenticity lies all the wisdom of life that longs to be lived. It leads us in the direction that is best for us. Life is happening for us. We are taken care of.

Thank you for being here with me, my friends. Thank you for the time you've spent reading these words. Thank you for listening. And even if we've never met, please know—I care about you.

If there's ever anything I can do for you, please, reach out.

With deepest love and gratitude,
Your Katerina

"Only the truth of who you are, if realized, will set you free."

— Eckhart Tolle

A Big Ball of Loving Energy

By Cory MacNeil

If the Courtyard Scottsdale Salt River Hotel was a coffee shop, it would be a Starbucks, not a Dunkin' Donuts. Before you reach the main entrance, you half-expect to be greeted by employees dressed like the bartender in The Shining. Heck, you might not even be surprised to see Stephen King seated at a table in the lobby, hunched over a sprawling manuscript.

Or, as in my case, you might encounter Life Coach Steve Hardison in mirrored shades, dressed in a suit, and holding a briefcase while he speaks with someone. After all, I wasn't at just any old event; this was the Ultimate Experience Conference! It was two and a half days of teaching and connection with close to three hundred attendees.

In the previous months, I had decided to be more authentic on Facebook. So, I challenged myself to post live videos every day for thirty days straight. During that time, I focused on creating content and being less self-conscious. Sometimes that meant hitting "record" and speaking from the heart. There was no rehearsing. Hardly ever a marshalling of thoughts. The aim was to be relaxed and not judge myself or worry about likes. I was looking to crucify my ego. Because of this challenge, I felt more authentic than ever. I was being myself and overcoming my fear of being judged by myself and others.

After the self-imposed live challenge, authenticity began showing up in my writing. One piece I posted, about a year-long desert experience I had, made some noise. I posted that piece on January 27, 2025. It chronicled my life leading up to and after my resignation as a pastor. As a result of sharing this story, people were touched and connected with me in the comments. I learned many people would celebrate our accomplishments; however, they're most willing to celebrate with us when we share our challenges and struggles! Here, it was wise to open my heart because it led to a connection with others. The people we relate to most are people just like us, those who overcame humble beginnings.

This post caught the attention of my publisher, John R. Spender. Ironically, I had wrestled with letting that piece become exposed because I felt it was a bit too heavy and not in line with my celebration of the importance of being positive and having a powerful mindset. In retrospect, I'm glad that I did! Had I not published that post, I might not be writing the essay you're reading right now! The lesson about the wisdom of authenticity? Stop apologizing for being yourself, and don't be afraid to publish your diary! In John, I found a publisher who is both gracious and patient.

I published the piece about my desert experience on Facebook after spending several days at the Ultimate Coach event in Scottsdale, Arizona.

Before attending the conference, I had set the intention to be a "big ball of loving energy!" While setting this intention, I wasn't sure what that would look like, but I figured it out along the way. I wasn't focused on what I was going to do. I was all about who I was being. My reason for setting that intention was that I had received much over the years and wanted to be a giver, not a taker, at the event. What happened next still boggles me to this day. Setting the intention to be a "big ball of loving energy" was one of the wisest decisions I ever made!

Another wise decision I made was to find out who Steve Hardison was and to attend the Ultimate Experience in Arizona. I first saw Steve on Friday, January 24, 2025, at the Salt River Hotel in Scottsdale, Arizona. Dressed in a suit and wearing mirrored sunglasses, Steve impressed me as tall, present, and confident. What does this have to do with being authentic? Seeing Steve, I was convinced that I was seeing someone who was being himself (authentic). This Ultimate Coach (me) was seeing with his own two eyes the bona fide, original Ultimate Coach (I refer to myself as the Ultimate Coach here because that is as Steve would have it! He encourages everyone who reads the book about him to read it as though it is about them!)

I share this to show my willingness to publicly proclaim my impression of what I saw. A part of me in the past would have been afraid to do that because of what others might think if I shared my admiration for a public figure. I had an amazing opportunity then to see him in person, and now to share publicly. It was a surreal moment. But the best was yet to come!

I had been interested in the Ultimate Coach for about nine years when I first heard of him. I say this because he was private and didn't do interviews. But he appeared on my radar. Fast forward about five years, and he accepted my friend request, and I followed the Ultimate Coach page. During that time, I won his Dog Naming Contest (that's right, I loved the name Hershey for Amy's Shih Tzu, and so did Amy and Steve!). And just like he loved the name Hershey, I loved Amy's book, The Ultimate Coach. I am telling you this because it's true, and I promise you that your life will be changed if you purchase and read the book and start sharing what excites you publicly. Again, just being authentic! Nine years of waiting were finally paying off.

One of the speakers on the first day was Stephen McGee. Stephen has a golden retriever personality and was very warm and interested when he spoke with me after his talk. During his talk, he shared a phrase that stuck with me because it was so authentic. He had lost his home recently in the Los Angeles wildfires. He said, "Lately I've been hiding." I appreciated his honesty. Although he may have been feeling that way, he was so real that he was doing anything but hiding. Unlike me at times, when I underplay and internalize struggle, McGee was forthcoming and vulnerable.

I had been kind of hiding that past year after resigning after twenty-five years in ministry. Hiding from myself, my family, clients, and friends. Although my resignation had been a godsend, there were still days of grief and regret. I had been burning the candle at both ends for years until there wasn't any candle to burn, and now, when I needed to pour back into myself, the super-pastor in me felt guilty at times. I was hiding. Not allowing anyone, including my wife, to see the pain.

Fast forward to the conclusion of that first day at the conference. I sat about three-quarters of the way back from the stage that night and glanced at Steve near the stage. I had two thoughts: 1) I'd love to meet Steve; and 2) I'll have all week to do that. The keyword here is all, meaning I can meet him at any time in the future that I want to. I thought to myself, I don't know if he will be here tomorrow, or even if I will! That is wisdom, my friend. Wisdom is knowledge and applied experience. In the past, I had waited to seize opportunities, and I missed out. In my experience, the moment is the only thing that exists! I'll talk more about that later. Suffice it to say, I'm glad I was authentic by standing up and walking through the crowd to meet him. Despite past disappointments with others, I found Steve to be even more dynamic up close.

In fact, Steve was as gracious and charismatic as I had imagined he'd be. I won't share the content of our brief conversation, but he reminded me of the importance of serving without attachment to retribution. He told a story that touched my heart about his early beginnings as a coach, and that story re-centered everything. And then he asked a question that still makes me laugh every time I reflect on it, especially based on what I learned about his servant's heart. "Anything else?" he asked. I was so unprepared for such a question that I simply thanked him and walked away. Little did I know that when Steve asked, "Anything else?" he meant it! I'll let you think about that. I'm glad that I loved myself and considered myself worthy enough to introduce myself to Steve.

It turns out, being a big ball of loving energy can lead to life-changing conversations! It also leads to other miracles, as we're about to see.

During the conference, I met wonderful people. Part of what made them wonderful was the fact that they were interested in growth and personal development. The following story is about one of those people I had the chance to meet and an opportunity I missed because I wasn't being authentic!

The person I am speaking of is Ankush Jain. For those of you who don't know Ankush, he has worked extensively with Steve Chandler and Steve Hardison. Looks-wise, Hardison calls him M.G., short for Modern Gandhi. But M.G. describes more than his looks; it describes his heart as well. He has a heart for truth, both in his own life and in the lives of others. Ankush is also a world-class coach. I had spoken with him via Messenger, but never met him in person. It was an exciting moment. When I first saw him, he was wearing a navy-colored wool coat with a wrap-around belt you can tie. Again, just keeping things real! Ankush is about as real as it gets. He's warm and kind and more than happy to give you the time of day.

What stands out in retrospect after meeting him is that Ankush impressed me with his way of being more than anything else. I was in the hotel parking lot when I saw Ankush walking toward me. Steve had suggested that I meet Ankush about a year earlier, and he had coached my coach, Nathaniel Montgomery. I had been waiting for Nathaniel to arrive when Ankush came walking along.

Nathaniel came zooming up and stopped at the curb, and said, "Hello!" and parked his red car. I spoke with Ankush while we waited for Nathaniel. If I had to use one word to describe Ankush, it would be H-U-M-B-L-E. Although he is chill and down to earth, the energy is all there, kept in check and reserved, ready to flow at will. And because I was not self-conscious and nervous, I could meet Ankush in person. It's one thing to watch someone's videos and read their writing; it's quite another thing to meet them in person and experience their way of being.

Nathaniel joined us, and we talked for a few minutes before going back to the conference. During that time, I acknowledged

Nathaniel's brilliance as a coach to Ankush, who had once coached him, and Ankush acknowledged Nathaniel.

That's part one of the story. Authenticity allowed me the chance to meet someone in the coaching community whom I respect. However, part two is that I thought of inviting him to dinner, and I didn't. Instead, I assumed he was probably eating with Steve or someone else. I assumed he probably already had an engagement, and I didn't invite him. Talking with him later, Ankush said he had been free that night and had eaten alone!

Herein is proof of what happens when we are inauthentic. We are not being wise when we have an idea or want, but don't act because we assume. The proverb is true... assuming makes an ass out of you and me. Had I been authentic, I would have perhaps had the rare opportunity to spend some quality time with a world-class coach and human being. That one's going to leave a mark for a while. Again, just being authentic. Just as authenticity can open doors, inauthenticity can close them.

Now that I've used the word authenticity multiple times, let me define it. For the sake of simplicity, I define authenticity as being genuine to myself. I'll add that it means showing your true colors.

Here is another story about what happens when we follow the wisdom of authenticity! Saturday, January 25, 2025, another miracle took place... I had the opportunity to speak on stage at the conference! Here is a snippet of how being myself allowed that to happen.

Meeting Steve the night before definitely hadn't worn off. It had been a pivotal moment to have that powerful conversation! The next morning, another encounter with Steve anchored our initial meeting. More about that later. On Saturday night, as the program was winding down, the chance to speak on stage was offered. In retrospect, I had not been planning to speak on stage. Secretly longing? Yes. I'd been a professional public speaker for twenty-five years, and listening to the speakers over the weekend kindled the desire to speak. Was I believing I would have such an opportunity? Yes! I must have because it happened. Why? My desire was genuine, and faith made a way. Besides, who wouldn't be courageous enough to act after meeting Steve?

There was an invitation for the audience to share if they wanted to. I accepted. From the time the offer was made until I joined a few others at the edge of the stage, I quickly prepared my short talk. Here is a brief and loose transcript of what I shared.

I spoke about how I had sat toward the back the night before and thought about meeting Steve sometime over the weekend. How I had then thought to myself, Wait a minute! I'm not promised that opportunity. Right now is my chance! I had asked Steve a question, and what he shared changed me. I shared how nobody is guaranteed an opportunity beyond the present moment. I then shared how I had the desire to share from the stage as a big ball of loving energy and how I realized that was not a guarantee, and I said, "I may not have the opportunity to speak from this stage again in the future, but I am here, right now!"

I stepped forward and challenged the group. "So, you've been wanting to meet Steve. What's stopping you from doing that right now? Or maybe you've wanted to introduce yourself to someone else, but you're waiting to step across the aisle. Or perhaps you've been thinking about calling someone and telling them you love them. Don't wait. Do it! Right now!" You may not have another day, let alone the rest of the weekend.

At that exact moment, I felt like I had stepped into my destiny; something shifted inside me. I've spoken with others who have said they felt that shift, too. My friend Bodhi Kenyon talked about this and even made a beautiful post on his website. Perhaps you've experienced that shift yourself already.

Immediately after stepping off the stage, Austin Conaty, a man I'd never met before, approached me and invited me to dinner with his friend Andrew Lampa. Austin has dark hair, a goatee, wears glasses, and is to be envied because he has a full head of hair and a stylish cut. Austin made me feel like a VIP as I came off the stage. He is also quick to find humor, and he often thinks before he speaks. I told them I'd love to, but I had already invited someone else (Matthew Adams) to dinner, so first, I had to see if Matthew wanted to join us.

Minutes before, I had simply planned to get some food and return to the Airbnb I was staying at, and now I was meeting new friends and being offered new opportunities, all because I was being authentic. I would also create coaching agreements with some exceptional people I met at the conference. I learned it pays to be genuine, and when we are, there is no predicting what is possible! I've spoken with Austin often since that time.

Andrew Lampa is tall, with boyish looks and gregarious. He is also a life coach who lives with his family in Michigan. For years, he had owned and run a diner before transitioning into coaching. We rode to dinner in his rented hybrid Mustang, and he enjoyed seeing how fast he could go from zero to sixty miles per hour every time he had the opportunity. We ended up going to a restaurant with mid-century American architecture and sat outside at a table with wraparound seating and a fire pit. It was the first time I tried calamari, and one morsel was an entire French-fried miniature octopus. I noticed the cool architecture, and Andrew said he had owned a house with mid-century architecture.

Then we zoomed all over the highways and byways and drove up into the mountains and stopped at a mansion that was being built into the side of a mountain. The entire city stretched out in every direction below us like a sea of jewels in the darkness. We laughed and shared stories. Soon another party of people joined us, and we tried to explain what the conference was about.

Matthew and I talked and laughed in the back seat. Matthew is a life coach from Birmingham, England. In my mind, he sounds like Shrek, which is cool, and he is also laid back and down to earth. Matthew spoke of how he had been coached over the past year and spent a lot of time working on his Document of Being. He even recited it to me when asked at the first morning I arrived at the conference. He also recited it again at dinner when asked. As we pulled up to an intersection, a driverless taxi pulled up next to us.

"Wow! That's the first one I've ever seen. Maybe I'll rent one to go to the Grand Canyon!" Matthew said.

"That's cool," I said. "You'd just better hope it doesn't malfunction when you get there, and the brakes don't work."

In less than a few hours, new friendships and connections were made. We were all leaders, open to possibility and growing, buzzed on the energy of being around other world-class coaches and leaders. We'd each invested in the conference, and it was paying off in Spades.

Speaking of friends, because I was authentic, I met and developed a friendship with another wonderful friend named Ligia Eberhardt Camara. We were already friends on Facebook, and I invited her to lunch in the lobby. She accepted and brought another friend of hers to join us. I learned Ligia had left her home in Brazil to live in Scottsdale with her husband, Hector. They are the epitome of what it means to be young and good-looking and have three amazing and beautiful children. As if this isn't enough, Ligia fully embodies what it means to be authentic! She is a very wise and talented counselor with a Master's in Counseling from Grand Canyon University. Authenticity, I learned, allows us to make cool friends.

Ligia is authentic in her focus on her family, especially her children. But she not only cares for her family; she cares for all people. I asked her permission to include her story in this chapter and asked her what she wanted to share. She said to pass this on to you: "You are unconditionally loved and cherished by our Father in Heaven and there's nothing too good for you!" Bam! Because I was authentic, I had the chance to meet yet another authentic human who feels at home in their own skin. Having a friend who loves and focuses on her family is inspiring.

Again, I'm also glad I chose to be authentic and invited Ligia to lunch because she has kept her word and been genuine with me. That's right! Some inauthenticity had crept back into my way of being. Ligia noticed it and pointed out my blind spot! Now that's a genuine friend. A little authenticity connecting with someone I did not know created an opportunity months later to be jolted back into authenticity at just the right moment. Talk about Divine timing! I will be forever thankful for Ligia's authenticity and friendship. We can never have enough friends who tell it the way it is when we need to hear it.

These are just some highlights of how it paid off and was fulfilling to set the intention of being a big ball of loving energy. The following story is perhaps the prime example of what it means to be authentic, and it happened in the men's room at The Ultimate Experience!

Sunday morning, while I was walking away from the sink after washing my hands, the bathroom door swung open and Steve came in, making some kind of spaceship noises (the kind a little kid makes when he's happy!) Before I knew what was happening, he walked over and kissed me on the side of the head, and said, "Good morning, Cory!" It still makes me laugh and smile, and it's a memory I'll cherish forever. Who knew using the Men's room could be so much fun?

In one moment, Steve modeled what it means to be yourself. Inspiration nudged him, and he acted. Did he second-guess himself? If he did, I'll never know. But I do know that was one of the most loving acts of kindness I have ever received. It was as if the Universe was reminding me that God knows my name and address. I may lose track of God, but He will never lose track of me. I had been authentic the night before, and now I was experiencing unconditional love at a new level. Thank you, Steve, for loving yourself in a social setting.

When we're authentic, it allows for more opportunities to be authentic.

Had I not had a genuine interest in finding out who Steve was, I never would have met him and learned all that I have. Specifically, I would not be the person I am today. Studying him and learning from him, I came to know the importance of commitment. And because I committed to being in Arizona in January, I could experience miracles I would have never experienced otherwise.

In my work with coaching clients, when they share disappointment with themselves, I help them see that although they may not have noticed, they are resilient. For example, if they're experiencing something difficult, I ask them how they've been getting through, and they are usually surprised to see that while they think they've been failing, they've been winning by taking action to get through it. Here, I give myself credit for showing up as a big ball of loving energy at the conference after a difficult year. That guy, in my book, deserves a lot of credit for showing up and maximizing the wisdom of authenticity.

Like Stephen McGee, we're never alone. And when we feel like we're hiding because of a situation or circumstances, there's no place we can hide from Love. Love, like Steve Hardison, not only knows our name, but Love also knows where to find us. And just like Stephen, Love puts us on the stage of life to love others and be loved.

True authenticity isn't about showcasing strengths; it's about embracing our humanity. We're lovable simply because we're real. As a human and a coach, living from love and authenticity isn't a part-time role; it's who I am, always. And you can be too.

65

One of my core messages as a pastor was, "People may not forgive you and you may not forgive yourself, but God forgives you!" And if the Divine can forgive us, what a great reason to forgive ourselves… right here, right now!

I'm thankful for people who continue to show up as "God with skin on." People like Steve Hardison, who have served intentionally for a lifetime. My coach, Nathaniel Montgomery, who has coached me faithfully for two years as of the time of this writing. Stephen McGee, who reminded me that when you feel you've been hiding, the best course of action is to rat yourself out and love the hell out of yourself. I'm thankful as well, for the entire team who made the conference possible, and all who attended.

I'm also thankful for Ankush Jain and his way of being, which can be summarized as "in service and love."

There's a lot of talk these days about authenticity. For some, it means that we just show up the way we are, but that's not authenticity in my book. If I show up mean or hurtful, that's not me showing up as who I truly am. Because that's not my true nature by birthright. Likewise, if I show up angry, that's not authentic. It's just not me. The real me is love. For me to be unloving is to be inauthentic.

The real me and the real you are so much more than what we do and/or say. It's not our bank account balance or our social status. The real me and the real you are not our job title or the color of our skin. The real you and the real me might even be someone or something that is beyond human sight and the third dimension. However, what we do or say reflects who we are being.

And the good news is that although we haven't been who we'd like to be, that can all change right now. In fact, today, at this moment, we get to choose who we want to be right now and be that. If we decide we want to be a writer, we write. If we want to serve, we serve. If we want to be a public speaker, we speak. And if we decide to be authentic, we get to be authentic—not later, not tomorrow, right now!

Who are you being right now, and who would you need to be to have what you want?

"When you show up authentically, you create the space for others to do the same. Walk in your truth."

— Unknown

Rising From the Ashes

⟶⟵

By Diane Pierotti

N eo ventures into the Matrix for the first time, recognizing
places he used to go in his previous, unconscious life.

Neo: God...

Trinity: What?

Neo: I used to eat there... Really good noodles. I have these
memories, from my entire life but... none of them happened. What
does that mean?

Trinity: That the Matrix cannot tell you who you are.

From *The Matrix,* movie.

"You're doomed if you do, you're doomed if you don't," she said,
"so you might as well do what *you* want."

My tarot teacher, a trained psychologist, medium, and all-round
wise woman, was delivering this indisputable and common truth:
whatever you do or say, there will always be people to disagree
with, judge, and criticize. Her words echoed in my heart, sinking
deep into my psyche, unlocking something. The little girl who used
to do as she was told, who didn't rock the boat, but tried to please
everyone to be loved, heard it.

I was an adult, still somewhat playing that game, toning myself down to fit in, looking for validation outside of myself. These words became a mantra of liberation towards greater authenticity.

Perhaps because I have reached this new transformational stage of life called perimenopause, I wonder when I have or haven't been "my true self." When hormonal variations so intensely influence how I feel and how I express myself, who is this "true self?" Who am I?

I am coming to realize that this elusive "authentic self" is something that is defined and rewritten through the twists and turns of life. Like heroes in our modern myths, Neo, Luke Skywalker, Katniss Everdeen, and Violet Sorrengail, we discover what we are made of and what matters to us as we face challenges and rise to opportunities to embody our truth.

I spent years trying to be good, trying to conform to a certain image of success. Until failure, grief, and motherhood taught me to surrender and showed me I was perfect just as I was. I am still deconstructing years of distortion, rebirthing myself like the Phoenix, and uncovering who I didn't know I was.

Authenticity is what is left when life peels away everything we're not. This is the journey of a lifetime.

The Early Years: Being Unconscious

I was a quiet and compliant little girl who loved reading and learning, listened at school, and played by the rules. I was at the top of my class, an irreproachable perfectionist of a Virgo. Perhaps, too, an impeccable product of what was expected of a girl.

My dad was quite different, and for a long time, he was my hero. He was greater than life, a true character, loud, ambitious, hardworking, funny, and irreverent. He worked for a United Nations agency and travelled a lot for his work; he even lived away for a few years while I stayed home with my mum.

He was remarkable, not only because of his strong personality and personal accomplishments, how he got to this international arena all by himself, and how his work impacted thousands, but also through his absence.

I was hungry for his love and recognition. Unconsciously, I had turned his absence into an erroneous belief that he didn't love me, that I wasn't good enough to keep him by my side. To turn this around, I strove to live up to his standards of success: education, status, wealth. I did my best to fit into that frame, to be "good enough" for his love.

I didn't always know what kind of work I wanted to pursue, but deep down, I knew who I was. As a child, my purest dream was to be a writer; specifically, a poet. I wrote from morning to night, reveling in my creative pursuits, playing with words and rhymes, naively and freely inventing stories and portraying my world. Later, my poems became a pathway to express my innermost feelings, using images and symbols—art—rather than simple, straightforward sentences.

Alas, as I grew older, I picked up the subliminal messages that art wasn't a real job and that I should aim for something more pragmatic, something that would pay my bills. As I chose to use my head rather than follow my heart, the connection to my authentic self began to crumble. I lost touch with who I was.

Looking back, I see that as a child, I knew my true north. I had an innate, built-in soul compass that I did not question. My childhood dream was meant to guide me. I put away my dream and imagined myself as a brilliant, high-level employee of some sort. A civil servant perhaps, like my parents.

My dad used to say that I could become an ambassador. That was his aspiration for me. Although becoming an ambassador did not appeal to me, I enjoyed travelling and living in different countries. Part of me wanted to walk in my father's footsteps and work for an international organization. This felt both exciting and familiar.

At the end of high school, I still had no clue about which occupation or what studies I wanted to pursue. I had always been a gifted student, so I did the reasonable thing. I enrolled at a renowned public college, the Institute of Political Studies ("Sciences Po") in Paris. It appeared as a gateway to a variety of job opportunities. I would have plenty of options at the end of the curriculum.

My peers at Sciences Po Paris were all excellent students, many from elite high schools. Sciences Po was a very respectable and esteemed institution, a tradition, a monument. I did not fit in, and despite working more than I ever had, I failed my first year.

I repeated my first year and failed again. When I saw my results, I broke down completely, sobbing, overwhelmed by shame and the belief that my future had ended. A kind woman noticed me and gently embraced me, whispering words of comfort and wisdom, "It's ok, it's not the end of the world, don't worry."

But at that moment, I couldn't hear her. I was trapped in a version of myself shaped by expectations, measuring my worth by someone else's definition of success. My view was limited to this definition, and I couldn't see the beauty and magic of my own inner truth. I didn't value my inner world or my authentic voice.

This was a major blow to my self-confidence. Suddenly, I was failing at the one thing that had been reliable: my identity as a straight-A student. This question haunted me. Who am I if I fail my studies? Who am I if I am not the bright student I always believed I was? Am I good at anything? Will I ever succeed at anything? A toxic belief germinated in me; I was not a clever student with a bright future anymore, but a failure.

The clothes I had been draped into had been torn away. I was looking into the void, not knowing how to define who I was. I had tried to make a "proper" and grand entrance in the world, opting for a select school in the great city of Paris, aiming for a degree that could open many prestigious doors, even to French embassies, but this was not my path.

What I didn't yet understand was this breakdown wasn't a failure; it was a breakthrough, a radical redirection back to authenticity. It would take time and healing, but eventually, I would realize that to attain a success that made sense to me, I had to be honest about who I really was. I had to stop trying to be who I thought I had to be.

Though I believed my life was falling apart, it was actually falling into place. This marked the beginning of my journey back to myself.

I had no idea what to do next or where to go. I was spiraling down, suffocating. My mum came to the rescue. I could live with my aunt and uncle in Reunion Island. My heart relaxed. This felt good. Reunion was my birthplace, where my maternal family lived. It was a safe and stable cocoon where I could let my guard down. I lived with my aunt and uncle for two years, rebuilding my self-confidence, reconnecting with family and friends, healing my spirit and reconnecting with my roots. I studied law and it felt both challenging and easy enough. I didn't feel like an incompetent anymore. I felt at home. Reunion is my "country," the land where I belong.

Those two years, held in the tender embrace of my volcanic island, became a homecoming to my authentic self. My aunt's unwavering affection helped mend the parts of me that had forgotten their worth. Nature, in its luxuriant and welcoming beauty, didn't ask me to be anything but myself. As I watched spectacular sunsets set the sky and ocean ablaze, gazed in stillness at the star-filled firmament and dived in the deep ocean vibrant with otherworldly life, I rediscovered the wisdom of authenticity—the value of simply being present, of loving without judgment, of serving from the heart, and of belonging to something greater than the self. It was there, in silence and simplicity, that I came back to who I truly was.

My aunt passed twelve years ago, and I will always cherish her kindness and compassion. She loved and supported many lost souls, including mine. Her work was discreet. She received no payment or public recognition for it, but what she accomplished while on Earth was profoundly meaningful, and it lives on in all the souls she touched. She showed me a different kind of success. A success that didn't need a degree, void of status and financial rewards. A success rooted in the infinite intelligence of the heart. She planted this seed in my soul.

Meet Pluto

In Reunion, I began to truly listen to my heart again, and in doing so, I returned to my authentic self. There's a quiet wisdom that lives in the heart, far deeper and wider than reason can reach. When I trusted that inner voice rather than the expectations of others, my life unfolded in alignment with who I really was. Following the rhythm of my excitement, I wrote some of the most authentic and meaningful chapters of my life, studying in England and discovering the wild beauty of Madagascar and Southeast Asia. It was through honoring the truth within that I began to live a fuller life.

I was in Pulau Weh, Indonesia, when I got the news. Pluto was knocking on the door.

It was a warm, peaceful, sunny day. From outside my room, perched on a lush hill, I could see the shimmering ocean. A common flying lizard was resting on the trunk of a tree, unaware of the tragedy unfolding. For once, my mum had called me on the phone. It was serious.

"Your sister Laure is very ill," she said. "It's leukemia. She might die soon. You need to come back."

I felt a jolt in my heart as the fabric of reality ripped apart. These words were impossible to process. I could not believe my beloved sister was holding hands with Pluto. How could someone so young, so healthy, someone I loved so much, be about to die? It made no sense.

In a futile act of resistance, I did not change my ticket to return home. If I had, it would have meant it was true, and she was going to die soon. Laure was in the hospital when she turned thirty-three. I missed her last birthday. I wish I could turn back the clock to be there.

For a few precious months, life was merciful. Laure and I wandered through London, her home, sharing our usual heartfelt conversations about love and life, conversations that always brought me closer to my truth. I was considering acupuncture, a direction that resonated deeply with who I was becoming. Laure encouraged me to trust that inner calling. In her support, and in those walks, I found a reflection of the wisdom of authenticity: honor what feels true, even when the path ahead is uncertain.

I fully believed she would heal. My sister was young, spirited, and alive in every way. Laure just couldn't die. She was undergoing chemotherapy and became bald, but still beautiful.

Synchronicities led me to enroll in a Chinese Medicine school in Paris. Meanwhile, Laure was doing longer stays in the hospital. And then, I got the call. It was our last chance to see her alive. We might get there too late. I anxiously jumped in my uncle's car, praying all the way that she would still be alive. We received a text message announcing her death, but I couldn't accept it. By some strange and very common psychological process of denial, I was still hoping that against all odds, she would be alive when we reached her.

But she wasn't.

When we got there, her figure was stretched on a bed. She didn't open her eyes. I stroked her pale cheek, and her skin was cold. Her body was empty of her. And I felt empty inside. Void of joy. Numb, and in the most atrocious pain. The inconceivable, the inadmissible, had happened, and it shattered my world.

I watched our dad endure the unthinkable pain no parent should ever have to face. For the first time in my life, I saw him cry. We moved through the motions of life, attending Laure's cremation, showing up, but barely present. We were ghosts of ourselves, each of us isolated in our own grief, unsure what to say, what to do, or how to be.

In that desolation, I understood how disconnected we often are from our emotions and their authentic expression, especially in the face of loss. We hadn't learned how to sit with sorrow without numbing it. That moment revealed a deeper truth: that authenticity is not just about joy and purpose, it's also about allowing ourselves to feel pain fully and to open our mourning hearts to one another so we don't suffer alone.

One night, soon after her passing, I was in bed when I heard a noise. In the kitchen, the radio had switched on by itself. I know in my heart of hearts it was her. The next day, she came through a song she liked: *You Are So Beautiful* by Joe Cocker. It was both a sign of her and an unforgettable message of love. She then visited me in a dream. I was surprised and elated to see her! We hugged, but she told me she couldn't stay, that she was busy in the afterlife or the everlife helping others. It was a bittersweet encounter.

Previous experiences had shown me there was more to life than what the eyes can see or what the hands can touch. I was practicing reiki and learning acupuncture, two modalities that work with invisible forces yet yield observable results.

My late grandfathers had both made appearances before, one in an extraordinary dream visitation when I was seventeen that influenced me greatly, and the other at my grandmother's deathbed. I smelled his cologne fifteen years after his passing, a scent I hadn't come across since. He had come to welcome her.

I had long been fascinated by mediumship, clairvoyance, and shamanic traditions, but when my sister and father passed, I didn't feel the need to consult anyone. Deep within, I already knew the truth. I knew they were still present, "alive" in another form. This knowledge didn't just come from books. It was a felt experience, a living truth. I trusted my authentic wisdom. It reminded me that authenticity means standing by the truth that pulses in our hearts, even when the world offers countless ways to seek it outside ourselves.

However, despite my faith and the signs I got from Laure, I was overwhelmed by grief. Knowing that life and love are eternal did not take away the pain. Yet, I had no choice but to surrender to what was, and in the abyss of grief, seedlings sprouted and slowly blossomed over the years.

Like an oyster makes a pearl with the irritant grain of sand that hurts its flesh, so can we alchemize our pain and generate something meaningful because of it. This is the gift Pluto left me.

I can now walk with others going through the valley of death. I can deeply sympathize from a place of experience. I can hold space and be truly present. I remember which words hurt me and what helped me back then. Even if our grief differs in some ways, I know the engulfing intensity of this pain. Death forever changed me, taking people I loved dearly, pillars of my identity. People who taught me so much.

Clue by clue, I followed the subtle thread of signs, exquisite winks from the spirit world that guided me toward something deeply familiar. As I connected with mediums and began developing my psychic and mediumship abilities, I wasn't learning something new; I was remembering something true. I had once dreamed of becoming a shaman, a healing bridge between the physical and the spiritual. In embracing that path, I was simply returning to who I had always been. The wisdom of authenticity revealed itself in each step: trust the call within, even when it defies convention, and honor the gifts that feel innately yours.

It didn't look like the prolonged stays in the Amazonian rainforest or the Mongolian steppes I had imagined, and I won't call myself a shaman, but I learned to walk between worlds, trusting my intuition and the subtle information piercing through.

When you receive evidence that your loved ones have not disappeared into nothingness, that they are still present, albeit in another form, it is like a window being flung open and letting the sunshine illuminate your darkened and lonely bleeding heart. When you feel this connection with your loved one, the very connection you thought was forever lost, something miraculous takes place. The invisible string of love is not severed! It is obvious, and your heart can start beating a little more lightly. You welcome back joy, hope, and faith. You welcome back life. I consider this a most sacred work.

During my school years, I had been so focused on logic and reason that I lost touch with the part of me that sees beyond logic. I found my way back.

My most profound experiences came when I followed the quiet knowing of my heart, the intuitive nudges, the sensations in my body, and the whispers from the spirit world. Each step was a return to the wisdom of authenticity. I adopted tools to help me decipher the guidance of the universe. Not only do I converse with my heart and with Spirit, I use tarot cards and astrology as a tangible system of interpretation.

This is my authenticity, walking between palpable and immaterial dimensions, led not only by reason, but by the shivers of my heart. I chose this path as much as it chose me. When I look at my birth chart, I smile tenderly; it was written in the stars, always meant to be.

Motherhood

I was forged in the furnace of death as much as being re-modeled by my children's births. Birth and death, the two most extreme edges of existence, shaped me more profoundly than any other experience could. Nothing else strips you down so completely and confronts you with the raw essence of who you are. In those moments, the ambient noise falls away, and all that remains is presence and the truth of who you are.

I had a precise idea of how I wanted to give birth. In my twenties, I read a fascinating article quoting Dr. Michel Odent, a revolutionary French obstetrician, about water birth, gentle physiological birthing, and the role of oxytocin. In giving birth, women undergo a sacred process in which a cascade of hormones like oxytocin induce a deep bond with their baby from the very start, while pushing the limits of what the body can achieve. Oxytocin is responsible for our feelings of love and plays a central role in orgasm, birth, and breastfeeding. In childbirth, oxytocin and endorphins create a non-ordinary state of consciousness, a trance in which women can open up, transcend the threshold of pain, and go beyond their normal capacities. Women are the gatekeepers through which life can come, and in these sacred moments we become superhuman. This can only happen when mothers feel safe and relaxed, and the body is allowed to give birth by itself, without epidural or other interventions that block the production of oxytocin.

This set me on an unequivocal path, which I strengthened by researching as a Virgo does! Inspired by this knowledge and powerful images of women giving birth by themselves at home, in the sea, or in the jungle, I was determined to give birth naturally, and in water. Water is the element in which every baby grows. In the warm womb of their mother, babies are comfortably immersed in fluid; it is what they have always known.

My ultimate fantasy was to give birth in the ocean, surrounded by dolphins. Alas, despite my prayers, my children did not have water births. They had other plans, and I had to reroute and follow their lead.

For my first child, I labored for thirty-six hours with my hypnobirthing recordings, plunging faithfully in the birth pool, supported by my wonderful doula, but I failed to have my dream birth. I ended up having a cesarean, the exact opposite of what I wanted!

My authentic self is a hippie, a tree hugger, and a mystic. I became a traditional Chinese medicine practitioner to support the body's abilities to balance itself naturally with diet, acupuncture, possibly herbs, and nothing else. My plan was never to abide by a modern model of giving birth with systematic epidurals, synthetic oxytocin, and cesareans.

I was grateful for the safe and respectful birth of my first child, but when my dream of becoming pregnant with twins became true, I was more determined than ever to have an intervention-free, vaginal birth. No cesarean!

I did a lot of research. My twins each had their own placenta and amniotic sac, which is considered low-risk and gave me confidence. Nevertheless, the hospital pressed for a caesarean. I was told that it was risky and my babies could die. I was told that statistics meant I was making the wrong choice, while also being told there weren't many studies supporting this narrative! I had to stand firm in my truth and trust my inner wisdom completely to push back against the fearmongering. I wanted my babies to be born the natural way. I wanted to give them the best start in life and I knew my body could do it. This had always been my inner calling, and I felt fiercely about it.

Women often feel let down by the medical system, betrayed, robbed of their power, and they mourn the birth they were never allowed to have. This was a fight for all the women who wanted to follow their natural instinct, who trusted the wisdom of their bodies against a system more concerned with profit and efficiency.

I was lucky to find allies who shared my vision—doctors who did not write numbers on a piece of paper, but looked me in the eye and affirmed they were there to support me the best way they could.

We had a successful VBAC (Vaginal Birth After a Cesarean). My twins were born at thirty-seven weeks, on my own terms, aligned with what felt right for me. With only minimal intervention and the quiet guidance of my experienced midwives and doula, I was able to reach this trance state that allows women to go beyond their usual limitations. My husband cut our babies' cord once it had stopped pulsating, and we were the first people to hold them.

It was the most amazing and holy experience.

I was guided by something wild and wise in me, something that knew exactly what was right for me and my babies. The wisdom of authenticity led me by the hand. This time I did not follow the opinions of others and the conventional path. I tenaciously listened to my inner truth.

The day after their birth, my obstetrician congratulated me. "All the hospital is talking about you," he said. "About your twins being born vaginally after a cesarean."

It was exceptional, because other women like me would have been discouraged and threatened like I had been. They wouldn't have found the support I did. I listened to my inner voice despite the odds, despite the pressure, the threats, and the challenges. I was proud, hoping this personal victory would inspire more doctors to truly see their patients and support their birth wishes.

My children's births were only the beginning of motherhood. Nobody had told me how much of a transformation becoming a mother would be. We give up our insouciance, our priorities change majorly, and we sacrifice a lot to the sacred duty of caring for our children: our sleep, freedom, needs, desires, and passions.

Amid the chaos of the early years, I often asked myself, "Who am I?"

I couldn't sleep or shower whenever I wanted to, let alone read a book or do anything just for me. When all the little things that used to define you are silenced because little ones depend on you, your sense of self can fade. Sometimes I felt like I was just a milk provider! Yet, in that turmoil, the wisdom of authenticity called me to reconnect with who I was beneath the responsibilities. I found little pockets of freedom to connect to my inner self, to my passions and values. It was hard, as every great transition is, but I stayed the course and found my spark.

Now that they are older and more independent, routines are easier and I have grown accustomed to my role as a mother.

And here I am going through another metamorphosis: perimenopause. This time, I face it with more maturity and serenity, knowing that once again, I will shed layers of my old self and what I thought I had to be to emerge anew. This time, I know I just need to remember the woman I have always been, beyond my changing body, beyond the masks and the roles, beyond external expectations and the stories I believed.

Like the phoenix, I will rise from my own ashes, stepping into the next chapter expanded. This new season is not about erasing who I was, but about embracing what is beginning, and this time, I know the wisdom of authenticity will guide me back to myself, again and again.

"There is no deeper connection than the one built on authenticity."

— Unknown

Authenticity: The Song of the Soul

By Jojo Tonnaer

When I was sixteen, on our way home from high school, my close friend Maurice made a solemn announcement that left a lasting impression on me. He had decided he would always speak the truth, no matter what. It was in his voice that I felt the sincerity of this commitment. Maurice already possessed a grounded presence and a sense of self, which gave him charisma and an aura of purpose, rare for someone our age. I admired his authenticity and level-headedness, and had always looked up to him, even when he was a scrawny, nerdy-looking kid with glasses that covered most of his face. I was not surprised by his decision, because I knew that, unlike me, he felt comfortable setting boundaries and speaking up for himself.

Maurice's parents had a busy photography studio next to their home. His father often called on him to man the shop, tidy up props, and set up the next shoot. After Maurice told me these jobs were taking up too much of his time, I noticed that he firmly stood his ground when expected to drop everything and help, even though his father had a rather short fuse, and, at times during these interactions, would turn an alarming shade of red. I remember one afternoon when his father barked an order up the stairs, telling Maurice to come and clean the studio. Hearing the heavy, rapidly approaching footsteps, I flinched, but Maurice calmly remained seated, pen in hand, focused on finishing the sentence he was writing. He looked up at his agitated father and said, "I'll be there in ten minutes, Dad.

87

We're just finishing homework." It was not defiance; it was authoritative but subtle. He was simply asserting that his focus and time mattered. His father did not know how to meet this kind of authenticity.

I reflected on what the consequences would be for me if I were always completely honest. I imagined people would get upset at my bluntness. I asked Maurice whether he would tell any white lies to make someone feel better. He replied with a decisive, "No." It was clear that he had thought this through and made up his mind. Looking back on this now, I understand that it was something he wanted to do to honor himself as well as others.

The irony that doing something that should be natural and simple seemed complicated did not escape me. I was willing to give it a try, even though I was worried about talking myself into a hornet's nest with no escape. What did that say about my authenticity? Was I more concerned about my own discomfort or the discomfort of others? The next morning, my neighbor's seven-year-old daughter spotted me in the garden, and she excitedly invited me over to do some drawing with her. I quickly made up an excuse that I had homework, because I did not feel like playing with her and wanted to go into town with my friends. The lie slipped out so effortlessly that I felt a pang of embarrassment. In that moment, I saw how easy it was to trade honesty for convenience and how far I was from living authentically. I also soon discovered that I would have to make an exception for white lies to keep the peace in my house after I upset my mother by telling her what I thought about the ugly brown and orange vase she had made in pottery class. I had not yet discovered diplomacy or the wisdom of a silent nod or smile.

Did Maurice honor his decision? I would love to have that discussion with him today, but several years ago, he left suddenly in the midst of a wonderful and fulfilling life. His wisdom and vision must have been needed somewhere else. He had touched many lives with his authenticity. When the time came to pay him a last tribute, people gathered in grief and gratitude. On his Facebook page, one of the heartfelt messages started with "Even today, Maurice showed us what love is."

Maurice taught me that authenticity fosters trust and that this is the key to meaningful connections that enrich our lives tremendously. I yearned to feel this sense of belonging to a world that he had embraced so effortlessly and had embraced him in return.

Authenticity is about knowing where you end and another person begins. Maurice knew that instinctively, but I had to learn it. Not having a sense of self, being ungrounded, and having low self-esteem, I was an easy target for bullies. Growing up, I was an extension of my busy, working parents, always ready to jump in where I was needed. I was a mother, cook, caretaker, errand runner, and manager with responsibilities that were often well beyond my age.

My journey towards my authentic self began on a seemingly mundane, grey and rainy day in England, when I finally found my voice and faced my greatest fear. It was not a dramatic event, but rather a clear and firm assertion that arose from a deep place of calm resolve that unexpectedly came over me. A flow of eloquence and wisdom followed that I did not know I possessed.

Nine months earlier, I had been thrilled to land a job as a receptionist at a beautiful boutique hotel. I had started all bright-eyed and bushy-tailed and was excited to forge a new path in life. My work would have been enjoyable, too, were it not for the owner, Mrs. Jenkins. She seemed to visit the hotel just to bully the staff, and I was her favorite target. She mocked my Dutch accent and scrutinized my vocabulary, hairstyle, supposed clumsiness, and even the make of my shoes and the size of my feet.

My employer's unspoken message was that I lacked the elegance and sophistication to belong in such a high-class environment, and that it was only by sheer luck that I had been granted such good fortune. On several occasions, Mrs. Jenkins sat in the lobby with friends, loudly lamenting the lack of "quality staff" at reception, while nodding in my direction. She told her friends about two unfortunate incidents with guests trying to check in, and how I had to make other arrangements for them because I could not find their reservation in our system, most likely because I was "too stupid to spell their names." I had always been too intimidated to respond. But that day, something shifted.

I had just finished another nine-hour shift and was hungry and tired. I was expected to work unpaid overtime because reception was understaffed. I was putting on my coat when the hotel's owner swept into the back office. "Tell the new girl, Jenny, that she's fired. She can leave now, and you will stay on and finish her shift." Mrs. Jenkins was already turning away from me, confident that matters were settled. To my surprise, my voice rang out, steady, authentic, and clear. It was loud enough to stop her in her tracks.

"I won't tell Jenny that she's fired. That is the reception manager's job, and I don't think she wants to lose another good receptionist. I'm going home, Mrs. Jenkins. I have already worked many unpaid hours training receptionists, only for you to dismiss them or scare them away. You then expect me to work more overtime because we are short-staffed again. I am no longer willing to bear the consequences of that vicious cycle."

Standing in the little back office waiting for a reply, I knew that I had connected with an authentic power and inner strength that was much stronger than any fear or exhaustion I had in me. I was completely calm and prepared for whatever was about to happen.

Mrs. Jenkins turned back to face me, but the angry outburst I had expected did not come. Instead, she looked at me, and for the first time, I felt that she saw me. This acknowledgement created a subtle power shift, which opened up the space I needed to have my say.

"There is something I would like to address with you, Mrs. Jenkins. It upsets me when you criticize me about personal things. I can hear you when you have drinks in the lobby with your friends and tell them how stupid I am." I repeated the words I had overheard, every single one of them.

I took advantage of the stunned silence to explain why things at reception weren't running smoothly. My tone was relaxed, almost conversational, yet I spoke authentically. I was concise and clear. As my words flowed, I became aware that I had captured my employer's full attention. I did not offer solutions because I knew that it was becoming increasingly obvious what the cause of the problems was, and it was not me.

I gave examples of how her overriding the reception manager's decision-making had resulted in time-consuming consequences. I told her that when she popped into the back office to answer the internal phone, the scribbled notes she left behind were often unintelligible. Since we were all too scared to page her to ask for clarification, the dinner reservations, late check-outs, and other changes guests requested were often not recorded in the system. I did not have to clarify that these were the discrepancies she blamed me for, because I could see from the pensive look on my employer's face that she was beginning to see things from a different perspective.

I concluded, "If you would like to remain closely involved, Mrs. Jenkins, I suggest you complete the training to learn the inner workings of reception. That way, you can make and alter reservations, do billing, and run audits. Otherwise, it would be better to leave the work at reception to your team of receptionists, and the management responsibilities to your capable manager."

There was a pause. When she nodded, it was both an acknowledgement of the truth and a quiet recognition of the courage it took to speak with such frankness. I realized in that moment that fearful silence could never give me this liberating satisfaction that came from authentically speaking my truth.

I walked home taller that night, not minding the rain. Something magical had happened, and I marveled at how good I felt; present and peaceful. Reclaiming my power had boosted my self-esteem and given me renewed confidence. In those few moments, I had unburdened myself from months of quiet suffering. I had spoken myself free from those awful, sleepless nights where I would toss and turn, occupied with the injustice of pouring my best into a thankless job.

Just the night before, I had senselessly ruminated over what I should have said after another sarcastic put-down. Watching the hours tick away into the early morning, I eventually became so frustrated with myself that I decided that I could no longer sacrifice my health and sanity by submitting myself to this torture. It was ridiculous, and it had to stop. I had to confront the situation. With my hand on my heart and tears pricking behind my eyes, I summoned all my courage and confidence to help me put an end to the bullying and stand up for myself. I said a prayer to surrender my anguish and thanked God for taking my burdens and making me strong. Exhausted, I finally fell asleep.

It felt nothing short of miraculous that, after months of anxious silence and awkward self-consciousness around Mrs. Jenkins, I had spoken my truth confidently, and in a way that she could receive. Courage, honesty, vulnerability, and compassion had been the keys to the magical, unguarded place from which inspired authentic wisdom flowed.

In dropping my defenses, I had been able to be heart-centered. This allowed my words to resonate with a beautiful simplicity. It amazed me that there had been no trace of the growing resentment I had silently been carrying around in bucket-loads for months, so much so that my anger had started to consume me at night. Instead, I spoke like a neutral observer. The message had been so concise that it seemed to have been carefully crafted beforehand. In delivering it, I had intuitively struck the right tone. This was how effortless it had been.

This experience confirmed for me the transformative power of authenticity. It had awakened a hidden strength that rose from a place within me that I did not recognize. Not only had I not lost my job, as I had feared, but I also gained the respect of my employer. By reaching a point where staying silent felt more painful than being true to myself, I chose to honor my authenticity. From that place of integrity, I was able to access the grace and guidance of my wise higher self.

Mrs. Jenkins realized that flexing her authority and domination was hurting her business and she stopped meddling, at least for the most part. In her heart, she wanted things to run smoothly at Astoria House. Our brief interaction in the quiet of the back office caused a ripple effect that was far greater than I could have ever imagined. It benefited not just me, but all the staff, the guests, and Mrs. Jenkins herself. The atmosphere changed so much that loyal guests would lean in with puzzled smiles, asking what had happened. They could not put their finger on it, but the hotel felt brighter and more welcoming. This was more confirmation for me that I had been guided by the higher wisdom I had called on for help. I had just wanted to stop the bullying, but instead I spoke from a higher perspective that included everyone involved.

If only I could find out how to access my newly discovered ability at will. I had to figure out the formula. This was my naive and impatient conclusion. I was twenty-three years young and hungry for something I had glimpsed but could not quite name. I just knew there was more to me, and more to life. I didn't know then that answers are found in stillness, or that embodying authenticity is not a destination but a lifelong path. This was also many years before I learned that embracing more of who we truly are involves first shedding what we are not. Back then, I thought that the point was to get somewhere as fast as possible.

For the first time, I became curious about what I had to offer. My interest in latent human potential quickly blossomed into a desire to explore spiritual development. I began reading the work of pioneers who challenged the frontiers of mind-body medicine. Little did I know that I had found a lifelong passion that would slowly but surely transform me into the vibrant, joyful, and confident person I was meant to be. I had changed the course of my life by listening to my own heart. As a result of discovering that wisdom comes from honoring my truth, living authentically became my compass and mission.

Gradually, my routine changed. Where I once filled my evenings with social outings, I started making excuses to stay home to read. José Silver, Carl Jung, and other visionaries became my companions. I kept this newfound passion to myself, partly out of a fear of being judged, and also because I couldn't explain the sudden intensity of my fascination.

Some of the more obscure esoteric treasures I unearthed in dusty second-hand bookshops were also, to put it mildly, unconventional: guides to developing extrasensory perception, accounts of near-death experiences, communications with Archangel Michael, and explorations of our cosmic origins.

I stopped my long runs and started enjoying walks. This was an important step in my healing process. Running had reinforced my pattern of disassociation. I could run long distances because I disconnected from exhaustion and pain, but I often depleted myself. My nature walks achieved the opposite: they helped me feel more alive, grounded, and connected. With more of myself present, I was able to absorb more of the fascinating things I was learning.

I sensed that I was onto something that would make my life more fulfilling, and that maybe it was something bigger than what I had envisioned for myself. It was certainly more than what I had been led to believe I was capable of. As absorbed as I was in those books, certain passages awakened memories with unmistakable clarity, calling me back to myself and asking me to face what was true, unfiltered, and deeply authentic.

Learning words like telepathy, clairvoyance, remote viewing, and precognition, it dawned on me that they did not describe mysterious and abstract concepts to me, but rather spoke of abilities that had once been a vital part of who I was. From my earliest memories, I saw colors and glowing light around people and sensed realities beyond those that physically surrounded me. These words were leading me back in time to reclaim parts of my authentic nature.

Reading about lucid dreaming, I remembered dreams where I soared with angels through star-strewn skies in exhilarating adventures, whilst knowing my body was safely nestled beneath my blankets. On the way back home, the angels would point out familiar landmarks so I could see where we were.

I had been so convinced that I could fly that I ran around the garden spreading my arms and expecting to take off at some point. I remember telling my parents that I could fly, but had forgotten how to take off. Eventually, I climbed onto the roof of our house, carrying a blanket I thought would make a good parachute (just in case), and jumped off. This cost me a baby tooth, which didn't hurt and didn't bother me, and probably a smack on the bum, though I don't remember that. I was not too disappointed, because what mattered was that in that reckless, fearless, and exhilarating moment when I jumped, I acted on what felt real and important for me to find out, even when it seemed a bit risky.

One early morning, when I was about four years old, I realized that I could also direct my dreams. I was dreaming that I was in the neighbor's house, where I would often go to play. My friend sat on the floor opposite me, and his dad sat in the corner in his usual comfortable chair, hidden behind his newspaper. Everything was as it always was. Looking around, I took in details that were so clear, they had to be real. I searched for an object I might move, some mark I could leave behind as proof that I had really been there. Instead, I followed my friend outside, and once we were in the garden, all of my awareness returned to lying in my bed. These dreams carried such clarity that I recalled them as if they had happened recently.

My mother became increasingly concerned as my unusual abilities began to show, especially after several of my stories turned out to be accurate accounts of events I had witnessed remotely. Her jaw would tighten with disapproval and unease. I felt the weight of her displeasure, unsure of how to make things better. I had no control over the things I saw. When asked the simple question, "Where is your sister?" I would see my sister telepathically and answer matter-of-factly. When my mother wondered why the mail hadn't arrived, I explained that the postman was chatting with our neighbor on her driveway. There was no effort involved; I simply shared what was real. I began to understand that speaking authentically, no matter how truthful or natural it is, can challenge the beliefs of others and upset them.

I became ashamed of my perceived weirdness and even scared of my paranormal abilities, which were met with fear and superstition. But in my dreams, I remained free, flying through the night skies, walking through beautiful gardens, or running down hills of vibrant green meadows full of daisies, with the sun shining on my face, in a place I now know is called Heaven.

Applying what I was learning in my books, I could see how disapproval and fear had made me fearful of my own abilities. It had resulted in feeling awkwardly self-conscious as a young child, and the underlying unprocessed emotions still lingered within me. They caused problems through the power of expectancy. I knew that this was somehow connected to the bullying I had often experienced, but I had no idea how to heal these feelings. Even though I was rapidly expanding my awareness of what was possible if I committed to being true to who I really was, I could still only access this new wisdom on a mental level. I lacked the compassion for myself that is necessary to stabilize and anchor deep healing. I was still too ungrounded to embrace wholeness. I also did not yet have the support to help me excavate my authentic self.

Because I had disowned my negativity, I struggled to grasp the meaning of shadow work: the process of owning and integrating our negativity while welcoming parts we have disowned out of shame or fear. I was unaware that I mostly lived from my mask self, which was kind, generous, and forthcoming. It wasn't that I wasn't kind, but rather that I had been conditioned from childhood into a self-sacrificing role. Inside, I often felt frantic and anxious, like a drowning person gasping for air. But I was so disconnected from my own heart that I wasn't aware that these feelings covered self-denial and pain.

Back then, unaware of the burdens of expectation I carried, I thought that if I lived up to an impossible, invisible standards of perfectionism, I would be loved and successful. I would be worthy of respect because of how helpful I was to others. Underneath the empty striving that could never result in fulfillment was a longing that had nothing to do with achievement. It was not just a hunger for wisdom. My longing was my soul calling to me. It felt melancholic because of the sadness in my heart. I knew that I had lost something precious, and I had to find it. I had yet to realize that what I had lost was the guidance and wisdom of my authentic self. I had abandoned and betrayed it so many times that it was teetering precariously on the edge of existence. My soul was wistfully calling out to it, to me. It desperately wanted me to grab hold of my true self and tell her what she had never heard: "You are precious. You are loved, just the way you are. Please come home." I did not have the words to explain these deep stirrings of my soul that guided me to start opening my heart to myself. Without knowing it, I had found the Path toward the Self, as Jung called it, and had taken my first brave steps.

As a child, reading had provided me with a sense of belonging that I couldn't find elsewhere. As I grew older, books helped me find refuge in my mind. Soaring through worlds of thought, I left behind painful emotions but also the grounded wisdom of my body. Now my books were helping me remember who I was.

It was a revelation to read work by authors who wrote succinctly about their experiences with psychic phenomena. I learned that at night, when the conscious mind rests, the subconscious opens up a vast field of possibilities. We can plant seeds that flourish through the power of the commands we give to the subconscious. This is what I had done that fateful night in bed when I had decided I was no longer going to stand for being bullied. I gave clear instructions to my unconscious, and my emotionally charged prayer affirmed a course of action that I had adhered to perfectly the following day. It was exciting. I had just discovered a powerful way to direct my life.

I enjoyed reading about things that I had experienced personally, such as lucid dreaming. I resonated with the wisdom that our dreams serve to make the unconscious conscious, so that we can integrate these aspects of ourselves and become more whole and authentic. I became convinced that Jung wrote from personal experiences with lucid dreaming, as with other psychic phenomena. I imagined him taking a break mid-dream to discuss the meaning of a certain symbol or archetype with the higher aspect of his unconscious.

I learned the hard way that authenticity is not given but chosen, and that it requires actively seeking my true self to not let others define my life. It's not always easy. Leaving behind what is no longer in alignment, including friendships or relationships, is part of the conscious path of growth, but only when done with the integrity of authenticity. Every act of integrity creates more wholeness. It also creates space for relationships that honor who we are, a deeper alignment with our true values, and the fulfilment of our hearts' desires. I fell off the wagon many times; this, too, was part of my learning. Life offers many distractions that are designed as temptations. I almost burned out in a job where the status, praise, and pay appealed to my ego. It took a betrayal by an even more ambitious colleague for me to see that a corporate vulture culture was not aligned with my inner values.

Like kites rise against the headwind, authenticity is often tested when we rise against challenges. Sometimes we need to measure ourselves against opposition, to remember how powerful we are when we stand in the wisdom of our authenticity.

Just like the nature of the universe is expansion, the nature of our soul is growth. Reading that in one of my books, I understood why I felt supported growing into my authentic self; it's in alignment with both the laws and the nature of life. Authenticity is integrity, and integrity is wholeness, which moves us toward holiness. Flowers never wonder if they have the right to blossom. Yet we allow ourselves to be conditioned into hiding our true nature for fear of "showing off," whilst it is from this authenticity that we blossom and shine in our unique beauty. This is our birthright and our purpose, or "pure pose."

The soul does not care for material success nor for admiration of the way we look; it only longs to express itself authentically and share this gift as a blessing to the world.

My heartfelt prayer is that you revel in the fullness of your sacred self, standing in the glorious light of your wisdom.

"Whenever you feel authentic and genuine you are headed in the right direction."

— James Clear

Leap and the Net Appears

By Jill Sawchuk

I had a *huge* wake-up call when I was in my early twenties. I was sent flying, in a Jeep, off a cliff, into the Mexican jungle.

We were driving back from a beautiful place in Chiapas after visiting breathtaking waterfalls. I was looking out my passenger-side window at the way the raindrops were forming little yin-yangs when suddenly Dani yelled, "Hold on!"

I turned my gaze forward. The road was suddenly gone—only blue sky in front of us. And then came the feeling of descending. We were falling in midair. Flipping, dropping—and then, *Thud!* We landed on the roof of the car. Suspended by our seat belts, glass shattered everywhere, five of us hung upside down in total disbelief.

In that moment of near death, I experienced zero panic. Instead, just a booming voice inside me, loud and clear:

Are you happy?
Are you doing what you love?
Are you happy?
Are you doing what you love?
Are you happy?
Are you doing what you love?

These words repeated, ringing in my ears, as we plummeted toward what should have been our death.

This encounter with almost dying was the first time I understood explicitly what it meant to listen to an inner voice. I could suddenly see, with intense clarity, the contrast between living a life driven by pressure and external influence, and living an authentic life filled with purpose and limitless potential.

I boldly and radically started following my heart. This chapter is my story of how I have repeatedly taken the risk of living an authentic life. It is a story about listening to that inner voice. It is a story about trusting those nudges.

Instead of having to be pushed off a cliff to wake up, I hope my story inspires you to listen to your inner voice and find the courage to live your life's purpose, guided by the wisdom of authenticity.

Source has a way of speaking to us. Have you been hearing the call?

As loud and clear as that message came through that day—and as much as it radically shifted the trajectory of my life—it was some time before I heard my inner voice so distinct and clear again.

The next time I noticed Source's guidance was almost ten years later. Dani and I were living in a small fishing village, running a beautiful studio, Om Yoga Sayulita. We were spending our time chasing after two young children, surfing daily, and sitting around fires with friends on beautiful beaches. We were in love. We were eating amazing food. We were surrounded by a strong and thriving community.

One day, more quietly than the first message I had heard, but still clear, I heard a voice say:
Maybe you should move back to Canada.

Immediate resistance rose up within me. Why would I want to start all over again? Canada? The cold? The rat race? It didn't make sense. Rationally, I couldn't make it make sense. Months passed, and we continued to live the good life in Mexico.

That summer, we went to visit my parents in Edmonton, Alberta. We were lying awake in bed when, at the exact same time, we turned to each other and asked, "Could you imagine living here?"

In perfect synchronicity, we both sat up in bed. There was no denying this loud message coming through to both of us at the same time. We both wanted to deny it. Why would we leave our perfectly happy life and start over? It just didn't make sense.

We flew back to Mexico and tried to forget what we had heard.

I couldn't. It was too much like that voice I had heard the day of our crash. And it kept speaking to me: *Book a flight back to Canada!* This voice didn't sound like an average passing thought. It came at me like a fierce tiger—unrelenting.

Two days after being home in Mexico, my inner voice shouted at me. Again, it was loud and clear: *Get out of here!*

I thought the message sounded ridiculous. We had literally just returned home. Why would we so quickly turn around and leave? Even if we were going to move, it would take time. "What's the rush?" I answered back as I drifted off to sleep.

The next day, a second, unbelievable, life-changing moment rushed into my life. We were hit with a "once-in-a-hundred-year" storm. As I watched the water level rise inside our home, I understood perfectly what that voice had been trying to tell me. I realized it was the same voice that had once asked me so clearly, "Are you happy? Are you doing what you love?" It was a higher force speaking to me, pointing me in the direction I needed to go to live out my most authentic life.

Very quickly, I felt that same deep clarity I had after our crash.

We were moving.

I could see my inner voice had been urging me to move, but I had been denying the guidance. The flood affirmed what my gut had already been trying to tell me. Our inner voice is always leading us with the wisdom to walk our authentic path and purpose.

That massive storm washed away the fog that had settled over my clarity since becoming a parent. Motherhood had triggered many of my old behaviors. Looking back, I can see how I was getting off track. I had started to fall back into the pressures of societal expectations and old patterns of dysfunction.

That storm helped me remember what it felt like to listen to my inner voice, my authentic voice and to trust and connect with the guidance. As soon as I accepted where it was nudging me, everything started to align.

Within a week, a yoga studio owner from Canada reached out and offered me the opportunity to join forces with her in a yoga studio partnership. A door had opened effortlessly, giving me a clear path to make this move with a sense of security. It was exactly what I needed to feel safe enough to take the risk of moving my family to a new country.

My fear and hesitation melted away. I was in awe of the way everything began to unfold. It seemed as though all the pieces were coming together in some miraculous, preordained way—every thread weaving perfectly to help us settle into this new place, right down to the house we bought. The realtor's last name? Breedlove.

Once again, I felt connected to the guidance and able to see the signs. Everything was falling into place. I was starting to notice a pattern: when I turn toward my authentic purpose, life feels synchronistic and magical. When I let the pressure of outer expectations get the best of me, life feels heavy and difficult.

It was becoming easier to discern the noise in my head from the clarity and calm in my heart.

We sold Everything we owned, moved to Qualicum Beach on Vancouver Island, and I stepped into owning a new studio.

As much as I was sure we were doing the right thing, there was still an incredible amount of pain in the process. I remember the feeling of landing with only a few pieces of luggage. My emotions were raw. I felt severed and separated from my deep friendships and family in Mexico.

As we boarded our flight, it was difficult to breathe. I had a big lump in my throat and a huge pit in my stomach.

I wanted to chalk it up to germs and stress. I was exhausted from preparing for the move. By the time we were through customs and reunited with my folks, I was convinced I had strep throat. I could barely swallow.

After a visit to urgent care, it turned out I was just sad. The doctor told me to drink some tea and rest. I followed the doctor's orders.

I gave myself a bit of time to feel my feelings. I admitted the anguish of leaving behind friends, family, and community. My throat softened as my emotions were acknowledged.

However, we were back in my country, and I quickly started to feel the pressure again. I began to take on the role of being the head of my family.

It was a radical move we had made. I tried desperately to focus on the positive. It never made sense to my brain, but I could feel it was where we needed to be. It wasn't easy, but there was a great school, and all amenities were within walking distance.

Qualicum Beach is a beautiful place, and there were many aspects of our move I could appreciate. We could still spend time at the beach; we were still in a small community, and we were meeting kind people at every turn. I was welcomed and accepted by my new yoga community. Teaching in this new space was going well. I was able to continue doing what I loved.

However, I couldn't shake the feeling that something was off. My inner voice: the quiet wisdom of authenticity kept whispering, urging me to choose a different path.

I convinced myself to give it time to settle in. I told myself, *"Things will get easier."* Week after week, I woke up with a weight on my shoulders, tired even after a full night's sleep.

I forced myself to say yes to invitations for playdates made by fellow parents. I sat on soggy soccer fields, getting pelted by Pacific

Northwest rains. I even joined the parent association at the elementary school.

We were trying hard to fit in. I don't know if I consciously recognized it at the time, but I was abandoning my own feelings in order to establish a sense of belonging. I knew something didn't feel right, but I kept making excuses—justifying living out of alignment with my authentic self.

Gabor Mate, a renowned expert in the field of addiction and healing, says we have two needs: attachment and authenticity.

During this time, as we were building our new life, I could feel that exact deep conflict within myself. It wasn't what I expected to feel, because I thought I had followed the guidance. How could it have been wrong?

Being back in my home country, I felt lost under the pressure to conform to what everyone else was doing. I was struggling to live authentically. I was torn—I wanted to listen to my inner voice, but I also longed to belong.

About six months after returning to Canada, I realized I had lost my spark. Since that crash my near-death experience, I had felt so alive. That brush with mortality had given me the courage to follow my passion and purpose. I had experienced the joy of living an authentic life. I couldn't bear the dull dread and exhaustion that came from trying to follow what was expected of me.

I worked up the courage and finally found a way to speak my truth. My stomach was in knots; my head was dizzy with *what-ifs*. This was no easy step—I was teetering on terrified. But I did it anyway. I told my business partner I wanted out of our partnership.

What will the community think? What might people say? Will I be able to support my family? What will I do next? Will anyone want to study with me if I walk away from this well-known and respected studio?

I didn't have the answers, but I knew I wasn't happy and I wasn't doing what I loved. It was too much "business" and too much time at the office for my spirit to soar.

So I stepped away.

I leaped, and the net appeared.

My teacher came to visit and said, "Why don't you just teach out of your living room?" Even though we had been living in our house for over a year, I had never seen this as a possibility.

I had a perfect yoga studio right in my own living room the whole time—gorgeous hardwood floors, giant windows looking out at the forest, and a cozy fireplace to keep the space warm. It had been right there all along. Being locked in my "responsible and secure" job had prevented me from seeing the opportunity staring me in the face.

Once I cut myself free from those feelings of obligation and oriented my life toward what brought me joy, everything I needed began showing up right in front of me.

This pattern emerged every time I listened to my inner voice—the wisdom of authenticity. Despite the twists and turns, living in alignment with my truth has always led me in the right direction. Living an authentic life has always provided exactly what I need. When I let go of pushing from a place of pressure, everything falls into place perfectly.

Contrast is one of the keys to recognizing when it's time to walk through a new door. With each risk I took, I became more confident in that little voice I could hear guiding me in the right direction.

I began to see the distinction more clearly: my purpose was always being pushed forward by joy. When an idea or opportunity lit me up, I followed it. When a project or process felt heavy and burdensome, I knew it was time to set it down.

It can be difficult to discern between the voice of the mind and the voice of the heart. The mind often rushes in with logic, clinging to familiar beliefs and trying to keep us safe. But the wisdom of authenticity lives in the heart, subtle, steady, and deeply true guiding us beyond reason toward what genuinely aligns with who we are.

Once I let go of my old ideas and allowed myself to take my work into my home studio, I felt back in flow state. This bold move allowed me to do what I love And be at home with my children. My heart was clear, and I felt a calm assurance that I was exactly where I was meant to be.

It seems that at least once a decade, Great Creator asks me to check in and re-align. At forty-five years of age, I was deeply settled into my marvelous career when I heard the next call to pivot. Apparently, living from a place of authenticity isn't a straight line.

At this stage of my life, I had grown quite confident in my intuition. When I heard my heart say, *Take your work online!* I knew I had to listen, but I still tried to deny it—just as I had when I first heard the call to move to Canada.

I was comfortable. I had built a solid clientele, and my schedule was full with both public and private classes. I was teaching at a few community places, and I felt connected and in the flow. It was 2018, and I resisted making another change.

It began as a little whisper: *Take your business online.* My mind resisted with a firm No! I had a long list of reasons why this was a dumb idea. I didn't enjoy computers or technology. I preferred a real, in-person connection. My work was thriving just as it was. Why would I complicate things by diving into the digital space? But beneath all the objections, the wisdom of authenticity was speaking with quiet clarity, inviting me to grow in a way that felt unfamiliar but true.

Again: *Create an online program.*
Simple. Clear. I heard it.
The inner voice. The wisdom of authenticity.

My mind retorted in resistance: "No, I don't want to. I am fine with how things are."

This inner conflict was familiar to me. I had watched the battle before—mind and heart pulling me in different directions.

Living authentically isn't a static experience. Living from the heart requires a constant willingness to be open to what wants to emerge.

It is the ability to adapt to the New calling. Authenticity requires us to take risks. It asks us to be courageous.

It is easy to get trapped in thinking we know what is best. We like to be sure. We make a plan. We seek comfort. We cling to certainty. When Source nudges us to take a step in a different direction, no wonder we resist.

Who wants to take a risk without any guarantee of it working out? No one.

For me, at this stage of my life, I had already learned the cost of not listening to this voice. First, my near-death experience. Then, a traumatic flood. Next, the drudgery of going to a job day after day that lacked joy and excitement. This time, I was smart enough to listen to the message while it was still being whispered. These subtle, intuitive gut feelings connect us to who we are meant to be. Those subtle whispers lead us to live our most authentic lives.

If I look back at all the other pivotal moments in my life, before those giant shoves, there were many little whispers telling me which direction to move. I was learning. I decided that instead of waiting for the louder, fiercer nudges, I would follow the guidance.

All through 2019, I followed that quiet inner voice and poured my energy into preparing my work for the online world. I didn't fully understand why—it just felt aligned. Then, in 2020, the whole world shut down due to COVID. I was ready to open up online. Tuning in to that quiet inner voice had led me perfectly to the wisdom of authenticity. This wisdom guides us—often before the mind can make sense of it.

I bowed deeply to myself for listening, and to Source for guiding me.

Even though I had a massive amount of gratitude for my new and feasible business model during COVID, I was facing a whole new set of challenges to living authentically during that time.

There was a wave of immense pressure to comply with what the government wanted us to do with our bodies in the name of health. This approach, being pushed on us, was in direct conflict with my own truth. I was at the peak of my career, twenty years into teaching and living a holistic approach to health and healing. Then, boom! The World Health Organization was suddenly exerting a very strict policy and trying to force pharmaceutical medicine on everyone.

I rose to the challenge of staying true to my beliefs and resisted the external pressure to conform.

The names, grandma killer, anti-vaxxer, tinfoil-hat-wearing conspiracy theorist, were being tossed around. I was certain I was none of those things, but it still hurt being looked at a certain way because I had decided to live my truth. I faced many judgments. My children were no longer allowed to play hockey or go to dance classes. We were not allowed to enter a restaurant or a movie theater. We were not allowed to travel.

Staying true to what I believed required many sacrifices, but living authentically was profoundly liberating. During COVID, I came to some powerful realizations. I was no longer willing to spend energy pretending to be someone I wasn't. For the first time, I felt confident and clear. There was no second-guessing. No resistance. There was no doubt: I was going to follow my heart.

The pressure-filled days of the pandemic helped me realize that even though it might be unpopular, it was worth it to be myself. Being me felt right.

And here I am again today. It's 2025, and I am living through what might be the greatest test of authenticity yet. At almost 50, I am being asked to start all over again. I have developed an enormous trust in living from the wisdom of authenticity—even when it seems terrifying to take the leap in a different direction. When that feeling of *pay attention* pops into the field, I open my eyes wide to see what Source is showing me.

About three years ago, I observed undeniable patterns with my family. I saw the dysfunction of my marriage reflected back at me through the mirror of my children. Everything I was seeing around me felt like a glaring sign pointing us to live into a more authentic version of who we were.

I knew I had to take a stand. I had to rise for my children so they could witness what it looked like to fully face the truth—to live fully in the wisdom of authenticity.

I spent every morning writing my heart out in my journal. I meditated. I asked for support from the Great Creator, and truth and guidance came rushing in.

I was sitting quietly by a river when Source sent me a powerful guide: an elder Native man. He invited me to a ceremony, where he told me my ancestors were rooting for me and were here with me. He reminded me that we are being held by many forces we can't see.

Through prayer, ceremony, meditation, and reflection, the messages kept coming: set boundaries. It was clear. I could no longer allow that which never felt right in my home and daily life. We had to face addiction.

Thankfully, the addictions that run in my family are just the ordinary—work, weed, and alcohol. These are addictions readily accepted by society but destructive nonetheless. I was being asked to really look at the truth. To get real about what I was seeing.

It got dark. Our house took on a whole new feel. Heavy. Serious. My family retorted back at me: "My new most hated word is boundaries!" I felt wobbly in my ability to hold them.

I faced pushback. Authenticity isn't always comfortable. Being held accountable forces us to confront parts of ourselves we would rather ignore. It was painful to see our dysfunction clearly, to admit where we had gone wrong. Admitting our mistakes was gut-wrenching. The wisdom of authenticity doesn't shield us from discomfort—it invites us to grow through it.

We spent the next year rolling in the real, raw mess we had created by playing out patterns passed on to us. I was determined to be the cycle breaker. I could not bear to see my children suffer from being disconnected from their highest selves.

That voice inside me kept guiding me: *Jill, you are supported and guided. Listen up. You are on the right path. Keep going. Hold those boundaries.*

When my partner broke those boundaries, I felt I had no choice. I needed space. I needed to take a stand for my children. I was being called to step into a clearer version of myself, and I wasn't willing to dance with any energy outside of truth, respect, and love.

To be clear, my marriage and family life were rich and beautiful. Dani and I had been together and in love for over 20 years. We still laughed. We still had good sex. We supported and loved one another.

But then came that voice: *Set boundaries so your children can be free of these old patterns and pain.*

On the surface, it didn't make sense to disrupt our entire life. The risk of breaking up our family was overwhelming and scary. Doubt and fear crept in constantly.

How could we make this work financially? I wondered how this might damage the kids if I actually took a strong stance and asked for space from these patterns. But deep down, the wisdom of authenticity was urging me to face what was no longer aligned. It was calling me to create space from the patterns that were quietly eroding our truth, even if it meant walking an uncertain path.

I did it anyway. Everyone was shocked.

It is incredibly easy to create a story and start to believe it. We convince ourselves we are happy, even when we have those pangs of certainty that we should be doing something differently.

I feel so proud of myself for having the courage to listen to this inner voice of authenticity.

Dani and I have just completed one year of being separated, and last weekend we finalized the order for divorce. I never thought I would be here at almost fifty, starting again.

It feels both overwhelming and exhilarating. This familiar feeling of it not making sense. This deep trust in what is unfolding. My connection to that voice inside me that says: trust yourself.

To follow our hearts takes courage and always leads us exactly where we need to be. Time and time again, I have been shown that when I follow my inner guidance, everything I need shows up at exactly the right time. The wisdom of authenticity is always guiding us from within.

Even today, as I move through these big changes, I see all kinds of magic showing up to guide and support me. I encourage all of you to tune into that inner voice. Tap into Source guidance. Ask your ancestors to show up and hold you in difficult moments. Don't be scared to live authentically.

As I write these final sentences, a hummingbird flutters and stops just outside my window. There it is again! The Great Creator always gives us signs—showing us the way to live our most authentic life. Even though it was scary writing the truth of my story, that little animal spirit showing up affirms it: Just do it. Follow your heart. Follow the wisdom of authenticity.

"Authenticity is your most precious commodity as a leader, and you have to keep it."

— Lance Secretan

Renovatio: The Wisdom of Remembering

By Alexis Godinez

I remember one sunny afternoon back in 2018 when the following words just burst out of my mouth:

"Who am I?"

I froze, standing still in the middle of a parking lot, like time had stopped.

I looked around at the people nearby, at myself, and at my girlfriend at the time. Then I said, "What are we all doing? Why are we even alive?"

She turned to me and asked, "Are you crazy?"

I didn't know how to answer, so I shook it off and went about my day.

Little did I know that that moment was the beginning of my transformation, one that would lead me to uncover my wisdom, my truth, and my authenticity.

I used to think that being authentic meant being happy doing what I enjoyed, saying whatever I wanted. That makes sense, right? I mean, wouldn't you agree that's what authenticity is?

But the truth is, I didn't even know who I was.

So how could I possibly know what being authentic really meant?

I was living through a false identity. How can any of us truly understand ourselves when all we've been taught is to have faith in something other than ourselves?

My entire life, I was unconsciously programmed to chase everything outside of myself, with ideas and suggestions like, "You need to do this, and do that, go to school, get a job, get married, make sure you have a good credit score..." and the list goes on. I was always chasing something outside of me for validation so that I could feel peace, joy, love, and satisfaction.

You might feel happy. You might enjoy life after accomplishing your goals you have set for yourself and experiencing the desires you dreamed of. But that anxiety still lingers beneath it all, a spiritual hunger that doesn't go away. A hunger for something deeper...

Until that moment of awakening, you live with false ideas of what it means to be authentic. You unconsciously mirror everyone and everything around you, thinking you have to do this or that to fit in, to be liked, to be accepted. You worry about how others perceive you. You try to become someone, without realizing you've always been someone.

But when the being within you awakens, when the true Self rises, everything changes.

You no longer live to impress; you live with intention. You're no longer reacting to the outer world; you're creating it. You were never here to conform; you came here to evolve and create.

When you realize the being you truly are, you have nothing to prove but everything to protect. Protecting your inner peace becomes the most important thing after the sudden realization that your thoughts shape your reality, and that everything you've experienced, the good and the bad was created by you through the misuse of the power of your emotion.

Let's go back to 2018, to that moment that stopped me still in the middle of the parking lot, making me question reality and leading me to reflect on my past life experiences to try and understand who I was.

During that period of my life, I was in a transition where I no longer recognized who I was. On the surface, everything looked good, I had the pretty girl, a taste of the good life and yet inside it felt like hell. That contrast forced me to question everything, especially myself, and it was there that the wisdom of authenticity began to rise: the realization that nothing external can replace the truth of who you really are.

I thought I was maybe going crazy, because I came from a happy and loving family that taught me to always be grateful and to appreciate what I had. Yet here I was, receiving everything I thought I had ever wanted, and still not feeling satisfied. It worried me. It confused me. At first, I thought it was normal, that everyone must feel this way, so I told myself, *That's life.* I settled. I ignored my feelings like everyone else and kept working harder, distracting my mind with things, experiences, and instant gratification.

The reality was that my relationship was falling apart. I wasn't finding joy in the things that used to bring me joy. Still, I pushed through it, convincing myself that more money would fix everything.

Then my life suddenly began to fall apart, and I faced a choice: keep living the way I'd been living, or step toward something truer. I didn't fully know what seeking God meant, but I knew I wasn't ready to give up. I still had dreams ahead of me, and choosing authenticity meant risking everything for a life that actually aligned with who I was becoming.

I started reading books about the mind. Since I was young, I have always gravitated toward Einstein's idea that we use less than 5 percent of our minds. I always imagined what it would be like to tap into the other 95 percent. That curiosity led me to search for books that offered understanding and wisdom. I began finding value and satisfaction in my life again, but it still wasn't enough, because I was still trapped in my old ways of thinking and living. I would have moments where I fell back into the same patterns, and those feelings of doubt, unworthiness, and fear returned. It was like I was fighting a war between the good in me and the bad in me.

I felt like I was living a lie. The only thing that could satisfy me was the truth, but I didn't even know what the truth was. I was walking around questioning what was real. But then, suddenly, an inner peace awakened inside me. It gave me the strength and courage to keep showing up every day, dreaming and hoping for a better tomorrow. That hope slowly turned into knowing, until I finally understood that it had always been me, that I was the one I had been searching for. It was always my love, my inner voice, that I needed to trust.

That wisdom of authenticity led me to reflect on what I once saw as the past things I believed had simply happened to me. But now I saw them differently: they were designed for me, shaping how I perceive myself and the world. I realized why I often felt like I was living in the past, present, and future all at once. And when I truly understood this, my life didn't suddenly get easier... but I finally felt alive, and full of excitement to live and dream like a child again.

Temet nosce is a phrase I drew and put up in my house as art. It means "know thyself" in Latin.

No longer did anything bring me satisfaction besides trying to understand why I came to Earth.

That simple phrase of *temet nosce* became a daily reminder, and eventually a doorway into the wisdom of authenticity that would transform me from the inside out.

It led me all the way back to the beginning, to the very first feelings and memories that shaped my life, the ones that created the ripple of thoughts and emotions that eventually brought me to the moment I asked myself, *Who am I?* Deep down, I had always felt I was more than just a human being, and that there was far more beyond physical reality.

It wasn't until I began the process of getting to know myself that I started reflecting on my childhood. I began having vivid visions and memories that felt so real, it was as if I were experiencing them in the present moment. That made me curious: How could something from the past feel so alive now?

And that curiosity opened up another realization: if I could feel the past as if it were happening now, then I could also create feelings for memories that had not yet happened. That insight filled me with excitement. It revealed a deeper wisdom of authenticity: that I have the power to choose, and that one of those choices is to govern my thoughts and feelings. I could choose happiness. I could choose peace, joy, and love and embody them from within, because I got tired of living a life where I depended on my outer world to determine how I feel.

All these questions began to awaken within me as I started to fall in love with myself, a process I like to call getting to "know thyself."

One question I asked myself was: What kind of life would I be experiencing if my parents hadn't had the courage to move to the United States with my brother and me when I was four years old?

As I got to know myself, I kept returning to this moment, feeling it as if it were happening to me now.

Let me paint the picture for you by sharing my story. I travelled to the United States with my mom, my dad, and my one-year-old baby brother. I was four years old at the time, and my mom and dad were twenty and twenty-four, respectively.

I remember saying goodbye to my dad's family as we boarded the Greyhound bus, leaving behind my grandparents, my aunt, and my uncles. I didn't understand where we were going, only the heartbreak of a goodbye that felt final. My Tio Juan handed me a small copper warrior to keep me strong. I didn't know it then, but that moment became an early lesson in authenticity, the strength that comes from honoring what you truly feel, even when it hurts.

Throughout my journey to the new world with my family, we were moving and grooving underneath highway overpasses and crossing a big river that separated the two countries. Remembering this led me to a moment that broke me with even deeper heartbreak, because this time I was introduced to the feelings of fear and abandonment. These two emotions are no joke to live with. I'm grateful that I was exposed to these feelings at an early age; I can understand them and love them because they are part of my story.

The heartbreaking moment happened while my brother and I were sitting on our parents' laps in the backseat of a green Ford Bronco with tan leather. This memory carries a distinct smell—the leather, a scent I can still sense right now as if it's here in the present. I didn't realize it at the time, but we had been caught by immigration, and we were on our way to a detention center.

I can still hear the officers speaking in English. I had no clue what they were saying, but I was curious and uncomfortable; I could feel something was about to happen. Yet I stayed calm because I was with my parents. I felt protected.

It wasn't until we arrived at the center that they separated us. My brother and I were taken from our parents, and even though I don't know how long it lasted, it felt endless. The heartbreak shattered me. I'd already feared I might never see my family from back home again, and now I was losing my parents without even a goodbye. That moment planted a deep fear in me; I was broken at four years old. But, it also became part of the wisdom of authenticity: the understanding that acknowledging our deepest wounds is often the first step in reclaiming who we truly are.

Fast-forward: we eventually made it across the border to the United States, the land of opportunity, after ten failed attempts and one successful mission that led us to a loving family in El Paso, Texas. They spoke only English, and it was there that I was introduced to American candy and the universal language of love. Even though we couldn't understand each other through words, we understood each other through emotion. What I remember from that time is laughter, peace, and, most importantly, feeling safe. I was reunited with my mom, my dad, and my little brother.

My parents were basically kids. There is no way I would have left my extended family at my parents' ages, with no money, to a foreign country where I didn't know the language. That sounded unimaginable to me back then, but now all I see is how courageous it truly was.

Let's talk about faith, because my parents' decision became my first real definition of faith. Their decision to leave Mexico City and come to Oklahoma was fueled by their faith-driven dream of a better life and a plan perfectly designed by God. This opened my mind to wisdom, the wisdom to understand my feelings and to transform negative emotions into positive ones.

I also became aware that I am a reflection of my parents. We are all reflections of our parents. Those experiences gave me the wisdom to find my authentic self. And now I finally understand that old saying: "What doesn't kill you, only makes you stronger." It's a hard truth to swallow, but it's real.

There was still more I had to understand about myself, more vivid memories that would take me back in time and show me that I had the power to create the life of my dreams through the understanding of Self. That's where I found the wisdom of God.

Through this experience, certain thoughts and memories started revealing themselves to me, giving me the wisdom to ask the right questions so that I could walk this earth as my most authentic self, aligned with divine truth.

There came a point in my life when I realized I wasn't really searching for success, love, or validation; I was searching for myself. Not the version the world had shaped, but the one I came into this world as: pure, curious, whole, and perfect just the way I am.

When I was twelve, I moved to Moore, Oklahoma. The first two girls I met at the apartments we moved to asked me what my name was. I said, "Alexis."

They laughed and said, "That's a girl's name. We're going to call you Alex." I went along with it. I didn't realize it at the time, but that was the moment I dimmed my own light, the moment I unconsciously chose acceptance over authenticity.

For years, I carried that name, Alex. Through junior high, high school, and all of my twenties leading into my mid-thirties. I lived as him (Alex). I adapted, I learned, I succeeded, but deep down, I was living slightly outside of my truth. It wasn't until later, through the experiences that shaped me, through moments of loss, faith, and even material manifestation, that I began to rediscover who I really was.

The Law of Attraction was the spark that lit the path, my authenticity, the destination I searched for. I once thought manifestation was about attracting things: a Rolex, a house, and the lifestyle that came with them. But I came to see that everything I drew in was only reflecting what was already within me. Each moment was guiding me back to the one thing I had forgotten: me, Alexis Godinez.

My name is Alexis.

Not Alex.

And reclaiming that name wasn't just about letters; it was about identity, truth, and power. It was about remembering the innocent child who came into this world knowing he was already enough.

Today, I understand that authenticity isn't something we create; it's something we remember. It's the return to the self we had before the world told us who to be. I am Alexis. I'm a reflection of my parents, a creation of the Divine, and the Divine itself expressed through human form.

When I remembered that, I didn't just find peace. I found wisdom. I found my authenticity.

That moment in 2018 changed everything for me. Life started to get good after I began reading Bob Proctor's books, Earl Nightingale's work, and Napoleon Hill's famous book *Think and Grow Rich.*

Initially, I thought that maybe I had shifted realities. I brushed it off as a coincidence. But I couldn't stop thinking about it. I knew deep down this new journey wasn't a mistake. Something greater was happening. My spiritual hunger grew. I needed to understand more;

I just didn't yet know the right questions to ask. All I knew was that I was getting exactly what I wanted and that things came to me in a way that I couldn't explain.

When I told others my story, about how my life was starting to look different now that I was changing the way I think, most people brushed it off as coincidence. They gave me logical answers and connected the dots on how everything could have happened.

I knew something magical was unfolding, but I didn't yet have the inner certainty to stand firmly in my new reality. I stopped talking about it until that certainty became real within me, because every time I tried to share it, people echoed back my doubts and fears. In that silence, I learned a core truth of authenticity: your path becomes clearer when you trust your own experience more than the noise around you.

Then came the desire to know what Jesus knew and feel what He felt. As I searched for myself, my authentic self, I had to understand God, and that questioning doesn't seek an answer; it seeks awakening.

It's the question born not from the mind but from the heart of truth itself. It asks, *Who am I really, beneath the noise, beneath the masks, beneath the story the world told me to live?* I've asked this question all my life, not to escape the world but to understand it. To see how every person, every coincidence, every delay, every dream, is a mirror reflecting my own consciousness back to me.

Like Jesus, I have come to see that truth isn't found in books or temples; it's found within myself in stillness. To live authentically is to live as the truth itself, to be so honest with your soul that you're free to express yourself without judgment.

The deeper I go, the more I realize it's not about finding answers anymore. It's about becoming and letting the Divine reveal itself through me, through how I live, love, and see.

Authenticity is about remembering who you are. This experience, which has now become a story, was an awakening of myself, revealing how I had lost my way for a time, influenced by my peers, chasing material success, and doubting my worth. Then, through the synchronicities, I was reminded that our desires aren't random; they are guiding us back to our true essence, to the authenticity of simply being in harmony with our soul. This is why I say that we are not learning but remembering the good times and the bad times. They have all just been moments to get our attention. In stillness, we can feel our way back to our heart, where our authenticity lives.

"Seek first the Kingdom of God," says Matthew 6:33.

Because the Kingdom is within.

The Kingdom is your state of consciousness. The God that I had always been searching for was my own awareness of being. I had always searched for everything outside of myself to fulfill me, to satisfy me, to make me feel a certain way. When I understood what Jesus said about the kingdom being within me, and how all of my heart desires he'll add on to me, I asked myself, *What does that mean?*

The sudden realization that everything that I desire is a state of consciousness startled me. I thought, *So you mean to tell me that what I want or need is not in effort but in assumption? And that it's all a state of consciousness that I must be, by feeling it to be real?* This understanding for me was what was leading me back to my authentic nature of being. This is the wisdom that was being revealed to me as I searched for God and myself.

Authenticity is perception. Behavior or personality cannot measure it, but only by a deep sense of oneness, by knowing the Self. To be authentic is to realize that you are one with everything and everyone, and that all of it is a projection of your consciousness creating your reality. To be authentic is irrelevant because everyone is on their own timeline, but for me, it's being logical. It is spiritual.

To embrace authenticity, you need to realize that you are both the experience and the one experiencing, intertwined as one with the world and everything in it. You are creating your reality from within, and the experiences you encounter are reflections of that inner truth. Authenticity is the awareness that all is one, and that one is you.

The wisdom of my authenticity wasn't revealed to me until I understood myself and the mighty "I Am" presence within. And as I continued asking, "Who am I?" I uncovered my true nature.

I am not my thoughts.

I am the observer.

I am not my feelings, and I am not my body.

I am the awareness behind it all. This is great!

Once you recognize that awareness is the divine observer within you, a veil is lifted. You see life not as something happening to you, but something being projected from you. From that place, everything begins to shift. What once seemed solid and separate is now revealed as light, as consciousness itself. The true manifestation is the experiences created by your feelings.

My connection to the wisdom that revealed my authenticity is rooted in a feeling. There is a feeling that is dormant inside of you, waiting for you to start looking within, because what you seek is never outside of you. What you seek is a feeling. When you seek the Kingdom of God, remember that it is already within you, revealing itself as an inner state of peace, clarity, and knowing. The subconscious mind is the bridge between Spirit and form; it is where belief becomes reality. When the subconscious aligns with truth, you feel the presence of God not as an idea but as a living experience moving within you. The outer world then becomes a reflection of the inner one.

The Kingdom is not discovered by chasing anything external; it is found by becoming still enough to recognize what has always been present within. Alignment happens when your inner state harmonizes with the truth of God within you, and life effortlessly mirrors that truth back to you. That is what I call authenticity, remembering that it has always been you writing the script and playing the role.

Authenticity isn't about expressing a self that the world has shaped. It's about awakening to the self that shapes the world. I didn't realize how deeply the question "Who am I?" would impact me, because my whole life I was never taught how to understand myself.

There was no rulebook. But as I reflected on my journey from Mexico to the United States with my family, I gained a deeper understanding of my thoughts and emotions.

And through that reflection, I reconnected with a feeling I hadn't felt since childhood: a feeling of pure joy, pure excitement, the sense that anything and everything is possible. The feeling that I could fly if I wanted to. That childlike aliveness was all I ever wanted, and I didn't even realize the answer was that simple.

The journey of life is a return to the heart. Our imagination isn't something we're supposed to grow out of; it's the compass we're meant to live by. Never stop dreaming, because the moment you stop dreaming, something inside you begins to die.

I'm not saying I'm right and you're wrong, but I challenge you to look deeper within yourself. Truly get to know who you are by understanding your thoughts and questioning everything, not to prove a point or be right, but to gain wisdom and understanding. Until then, walking this earth without being your authentic self is a waste of your personality.

This journey we call life is an endless path of self-discovery. We have to love the journey as we travel through it. There is no right or wrong, only what you give power to. As you discover your authenticity, life becomes a blank canvas, and you become the brush.

No longer will you paint a picture from the personas you created to make yourself feel like you belong. You become the creator, living in harmony with God's law. Blessed is the man who delights in the law, for all that he does, he shall prosper. You're the law, you're lord of your life. That's what the wisdom of authenticity revealed to me.

"Authenticity: The courage to be yourself."

— Unknown

Telepathy, Presence, and the Hygiene of Truth

—◦◦◦◦—

By Kat Van Note

There is no future. There is no past. There is no day. Just this moment. This truth doesn't live in your mind. It breathes in your body, in your presence. Before sleep. Upon waking. It is a return. A ritual. A remembering.

Because the moment you open your eyes or drift into dreams, the world comes to write on your window. Fear. Expectations. Stories. Old threads. They will all try to hijack your senses. And in that hijack, the signal distorts.

Clean Senses = Clear Signal.

What many call "thought" is often not thought at all. It's residue—limbic feedback loops generated by trauma, memory, and learned survival. Thought, in this way, is a sensory echo. It's a scrambled pulse from a system trained to seek threat before truth. But telepathy? True telepathy is not born of mind; it's born of presence. And presence is a wisdom of authenticity.

Presence is an awareness of an electronic exchange of endocrine pulses. A transmission of resonant, harmonic packets of awareness that travel from your sensory system into the Higgs field, and are picked up by another's clean resonance, reversed through their chakras, endocrine, limbic systems and finally felt. This isn't a metaphor. This is a mechanism.

And learning this didn't come to me in theory. It came through the unraveling of illusion, over years of deep grief and sacred solitude. I have walked with suicide, betrayal, and loneliness so deep it felt cellular. I was full of love I couldn't receive. Like a lotus leaf repelling water, my cells resisted the experience of being held, because I never knew what holding love felt like.

I buried rage and called it peace. I hid my voice and called it humility. I neutered relationships and called that devotion. I withheld from myself, I withheld from the world, and called that spiritual.

It wasn't. It was survival masquerading as virtue fear dressed in grace. But the body doesn't lie. And the soul never forgets our true authentic frequency.

Learn to Be the Ashram

It's all about self-discovery.

Being around reactive people, telepathy naturally drives you into attunement with their resonance. If they are disharmonic, our exchange becomes disharmonic static.

Unraveling from disharmony requires finding the quiet stillness of your own infinite and authentic frequency—your signal. This is a skill allowing your beingness in the world yet not harmonically touched by it, even when the static pulls you into participation.

Once you experience and know your authentic signal, allow yourself to remember, "This is my infinite authentic signature that chose to come here."

Holding this truth activates memory centers in your limbic system to let go of the past, which is no longer happening. Your body relaxes and begins to breathe from your cells in clear quantum exchange with the field.

You become One with All of Nature.
One with Atum.
One with Adam.
One with the atoms of your body.

Conscious of your authentic and infinite signal, you experience all atoms that form the world around you.

The Spiral of Presence

You think you are standing still, but in truth, you are moving— spiraling—through space at 2.1 million kilometers per hour (1.3 million miles per hour). You are not merely orbiting the sun, but corkscrewing through the cosmos, pulled forward by a star as it hurls itself through the Milky Way at 828,000 kilometers per hour (514,000 miles per hour).

If you were to mark your exact position in space right now and return to it in twenty-four hours, you would find yourself 57.3 million kilometers away (35.6 million miles).

The entire Milky Way is also in motion, racing at 2.1 million kilometers per hour toward a gravitational anomaly so powerful it's drawing entire clusters of galaxies into its pull.

This cosmic reality liberates us from the illusion of permanence. The past didn't just happen; it happened trillions of miles ago in space. Let that hit you. You are not in the same place, not even close. The past is not here. It can't be. And every situation that has veiled your authenticity, covered your presence, is long gone.

Come back to your wisdom. Pull your awareness back into your body. Into now. Because this is where you are.

Pain and fear leave you separated from reality and in a state of limbo. Stuck in memory. Caught in a loop of non-reality by the memories stored in your limbic brain and endocrine system, trapped in a false narrative outside of reality and the cosmic flow of matter.

In other words, our limbic system is not just a receptor for fear. It is the powerhouse of creation. It is the core of our chakra system, our integration into the Higgs field. It's how we transmute light into matter, how we manifest our thoughts. The place where our infinite connection meets the core of our physical matter through all dimensions of time and space.

But to harness that power, you must strip away the scripts of history—the inherited trauma loops, the borrowed identities, the outdated roles. Only then can you hear your own signal from Source. Attune to that frequency. Align your presence to your infinite connection through the dimensional spheres.

For me, living in deep isolation without meaningful human connection, it was the silence that opened the stars, aligned my body, and awakened this authentic truth of what it means to be human.

I began reaching toward the infinite, toward the cosmic field, and asked the essential questions: Why?
What is the purpose of this life?

The answers came not as words, but as knowing. They bubbled up from deep within, where my questioning met my soul, and my soul communed with the Infinity of Nature. Of space. Of stars. Of faraway galaxies and dimensions that exist beyond death and life.

This communion became my bedrock. It rooted me deeper than any doctrine could. Because at the core of authenticity is true Nature. And within Nature is the truth about being human.

The value of life revealed itself not through philosophy but through systems; the interwoven fields of space, light, and resonance. I saw how everything connects to create a field that responds to the vibrational frequency we carry.

And here lies another wisdom of authenticity: When we hold thoughts, emotions, and a vibration that is true to who we are, our field aligns with life itself.

Authenticity becomes more than a virtue; it becomes a vibration. A way of participating in the weave of reality that is coherent, clear, and connected.

We are held, cradled in these fields. Ancient mentors surround us, not only in myth and memory but also in physics; the heliosphere, the atmosphere, the layered dimensions that form the invisible cradles of our transformation. And this is our choice.

Remove all humans from Earth for just a moment. What remains?

The planets, in motion. Our great comet Earth, spiraling through space. The Milky Way—a star river turning through the dark. The deep-space zodiac, the star maps our ancestors read like scripture.

The quantum fields. Packets of slowed light, photon information, forming matter for the briefest moment. Even your thought has weight, detectable by brain scan. Measurable because thought carries mass.

We are not just electric and magnetic beings bumping into each other. We are interacting with spheres of information.
The atmosphere.
The heliosphere.
The galactic sphere.
The universal sphere.

And beyond them, spheres we haven't yet conceived. Spheres beyond spheres. Dimensions within dimensions. Inside each, there are billions of light packets and photon codes of vibration. Each one is showing us how to return to ourselves. How to reclaim our true human Nature.

Like an Oak tree, which does nothing but fully become itself, we too can choose a life of radiant growth. A life tuned to receive light. A life directed by resonance. A life of deliberate expansion into the spheres of creation waiting for us to arrive.

Authenticity means I am aware of my ripple. It means I don't project my unfinished story onto others. I amplify coherence, not confusion. I remember I am a mirror too. And that which I mirror has consequence.
So, I practice:
Stillness.
Listening.
Attunement.

Because in every moment, we are tipping one another toward clarity or distortion. Toward awakening or reaction. Toward truth or noise. And it begins not with optimization. Not with intellect.

But with orientation. Presence. Because in the end, whether in the glow of a screen or the eyes of a beloved, we are all just trying to see ourselves clearly enough to return home.

The Razor's Edge of True Presence

A poem to Self
Raw emotion hijacks attention.
Fear.
Flight.
The primal pull to scan for threat.
It's ancient. It's wired for survival.
But in that moment, you lose your signal.
Because authenticity doesn't flinch.
Authenticity moves in connection with nature.
Authenticity lets presence emerge naturally from the senses.
You trust you are fully enough

to handle whatever arises, when it actually arises, not in the
imagined future or past loop.
Every new person, every new space, is not the past.
It only feels like it when your limbic system time-travels.
Come back.
To your breath.
To the you who sees, not reacts.
To the infinite, not the instinctual.
Because when you process fear inside yourself without authenticity,
your telepathic field vibrates that frequency—
and others pick it up.
They don't know why they feel unsafe,
why their fear is triggered,
why they start to act out the very threat you were trying to manage
silently inside you.
This is the paradox:
trying to protect others from fear, without clearing your own, can
actually spread it.
But when you root within yourself, into presence,
your field says: "This space is safe."
And others regulate without knowing why.
You lead by how clean your presence is.
This is the real mastery.
This is your sacred nervous system clearing your senses.
Priming your vibration in preparation for authenticity.
And you are already walking this path.

Being Authentic is Not a Performance

It's the willingness to walk back through your own illusion, barefoot. It's letting the self you abandoned millions of moments ago know: I am coming back for you. To be authentic is to return to the root "I"—not the role, not the ego's compensation, not the child who learned to earn love, but the one who remembers.

The one who burns at the altar of integrity, no matter the cost.

The world teaches us to perform. To be palatable. To succeed. But not to sit still. Not to feel the ache. Not to breathe our presence into the places of shame, silence, and grief. We were taught how to produce but not how to be.

And from that fracture, we default. To the partner. The guru. The retreat. The certification. The god who still looks like our father. To the algorithm, the brand, the political binary. We defer our truth in the name of a "greater good" while withholding the very medicine that would set us free. But withholding is the root of separation, not from each other, but from our authentic Self.

I've spent years learning this. Through losing everything. Through watching people I love die. Through building sanctuaries and seeing them used, taken, misunderstood. Through loving with no place to pour it. Through being called wise while still aching like a child inside.

Every time I lost my center, I came back. To the breath. To the body. To the Now. Because the only place authenticity lives is in the unfiltered now.

So yes, raw emotion hijacks attention. Fear pulls you into stories. Threat hijacks your field. But authenticity doesn't flinch. Authenticity doesn't perform.

Authentic Presence is the Hygiene of Truth

And that hygiene is radical. Because when your presence is clean, your telepathic field becomes clear. You stop broadcasting loops. You stop outsourcing truth. You return to a signal so strong the world cannot help but respond.

From the earliest whispers of childhood, we are subtly and overtly taught to mold ourselves to fit the world's expectations. Family roles, gender norms, religious doctrines, educational systems, and societal rules form a complex web of conditioning. Each layer of conditioning obscures our authentic selves, like veils placed over a radiant light.

I recall the suffocating weight of those expectations, feeling like a chameleon, constantly shifting to avoid conflict or judgment. The more I adapted, the further I drifted from the core of who I am.

The most profound moments of growth came when I allowed myself to stand still and listen to the inner voice that had been muffled for so long.

Rediscovering authenticity isn't about adding anything new. It's about peeling away the layers that never truly belonged to us. It's a process of realizing the essence of who we are has always been there, waiting to be acknowledged and embraced.

Through this journey, we don't become something new. We rediscover the powerful, authentic being we've always been. And in that discovery, we find a freedom and fulfillment that no external validation can ever match.

It's a process of peeling back those layers of "should" and "must," of discarding the armor we've built to protect ourselves from judgment and fear. It means confronting the deeply ingrained fears of social alienation, failure, or disappointing those we love.

This isn't a path of adding more. It's a path of shedding, of going inward, and trusting that beneath the layers lies a self already whole and worthy.

For me, the most transformative moments came when I allowed myself to pause and listen to that quiet inner voice that had been stifled for so long. It wasn't about becoming someone new but returning to the essence of who I'd always been.

It's a journey that reveals the powerful, authentic being that's been there all along.

Authenticity is a Revolution

It's the reclaiming of your senses, your endocrine truth, your quantum signal. It's you, tuned to your own frequency, standing in a world of noise and saying, "I will not abandon myself." You don't need to know where it will lead. You only need to be there, fully. In your window-clear presence. In your Now. And when you do that, when you choose yourself unapologetically, fiercely, kindly—you become clear. You become medicine. You become Creator. This isn't theory. This is lived.

Every reinvention of myself forced me to let go of attachments to the vision of my life. Each incoherent signal became transformed into authenticity; like the melting of a caterpillar's form into organic gooey material, then rebirthed.

I created safe spaces to live and time for freedom to integrate my physical body (sensory, limbic, and endocrine) with my non-physical body (chakra, intuitive, and authentic). I moved out of old patterns and social structures to locate the inner dimension within, beyond mundane life.

It is here that the death doula of authenticity awakens the center-point where inner and outer awareness merge into an inter-dimensional system.

The Center Point - I AM

To uncover our authentic Self, we need to understand the interplay between the "I" and the "Am."

The "I" is the timeless, infinite frequency: What has always been. What will ever be. What exists now. The "Am" is our physical, present experience, the tangible manifestation of that infinite frequency in this life. The journey to authenticity involves recognizing and harmonizing these two aspects of Self.

The "I" has existed forever, a consciousness connected to multiple levels of existence, physical, emotional, mental, and quantum. It is the observer and the eternal presence. The "Am" is the expression of that consciousness in the here and now, interacting with the external world.

To achieve authenticity, it's helpful to center our consciousness in unity of the "I" and the "Am," allowing the timeless Self to inform and align the present experience. The "I" observes the external life, and the "Am" interacts with it, creating a feedback loop of human experience.

That feedback then returns through us into the field of our infinite Self, still connected to all that is through infinite dimensions. The "All is" interacts with it, creating a feedback loop of conscious expansion.

When we notice both the "I" and the "Am" simultaneously, we align our inner and outer choices with our true essence.

In ancient teachings about the philosopher's stone, the mysteries alluded to in various spiritual traditions, and the questions of quantum physics all seem to converge on this point: The true nature of consciousness is both infinite and present, a seamless connection across all layers of experience.

By grasping the infinite "I" and merging it with the "Am" of our current life, we find the true center point of authenticity. This alignment allows us to navigate life with clarity, purpose, and integrity, fully integrating the eternal and the present into our choices.

The Journey Inward

Often hidden beneath layers of indoctrination, the path to this sacred inner point is as ancient as the wisdom traditions themselves.

My foundational indoctrination was deeply rooted in religion, where the concept of King Solomon's Temple was central. Initially, it represented a literal structure, a place of worship and divine connection. But as I sought to break free from the confines of dogma, I began to see it as a metaphor for the inward journey, a map to the inner sanctum of the authentic Self.

King Solomon's Temple, with its progression through outer courts into the Holy of Holies, mirrors the journey inward through layers of consciousness.

This concept isn't unique to one tradition. Ancient Egyptian temples also guided initiates through successive gates, each step an invitation to shed another layer of the external world and move closer to the divine spark within.

This inward path is echoed in Hermetic teachings, where the journey inward leads to the "refiner's fire," the transformative force that reveals the philosopher's stone within ourselves.

Using the religious framework that once confined me, I found a way out.

By reinterpreting these symbols, I realized that the true "kingdom" was never an external place but an inner state of being. The gates of the temple represented stages of inner work, each one a deeper dive into self-awareness and authenticity.

The philosopher's stone, the ultimate symbol of transformation and enlightenment, isn't found in the external world but within the depths of our own consciousness. It's the realization that everything we seek externally, wisdom, peace, fulfillment, has been within us all along.

By embracing this inward journey, we not only free ourselves from the confines of indoctrination but also unlock the infinite potential that lies at the heart of our being. It's a return to the source, a homecoming to the self, where we find that the mystery is, and always has been, within us.

By embracing this inward journey, we not only free ourselves from the confines of indoctrination but also unlock the infinite potential that lies at the heart of our being.

This journey inward is ultimately a return to the pure essence of "I Am," the fundamental recognition of our own existence, the childlike purity of excitement for experience and expansion.

In this state, we understand that the mysteries are not external or distant; they are the very fabric of our existence.

The "I Am" is the core truth, the unchanging center from which all authenticity and wisdom flow. It's a homecoming to the self, where we realize that we are, and always have been, the embodiment of that sempiternal "I Am."

With Childlike Curiosity

I never stopped asking myself, "Why?" The eagerness to discover the purpose of life occurred when I was eleven years old and I began asking the stars (or the living structure of ancient memories) just what is occurring and why I was in the middle of such a life. The accumulated wisdom of decades asking and unfolding is this: Asking "Why?" reveals each key that opens every gate inward. It's the quiet hammer that chips at the walls we didn't know we built.

Every time you seek "why" from the infinite source of Self you drop deeper from the surface complaint, to the hidden ache, to the inherited story, to the unconscious rule, to the still point.

At the still point, your center point of erupting signal, there are no more questions, only sensory presence. Your authentic nature reveals itself in sensory awareness of both dimensions of Self.

The ancients encoded it in myths and temples. Buddha sat beneath the Bodhi tree asking nothing, but having already asked "why" so purely, so relentlessly, that the final veil dissolved. Because, when the "why" isn't about blame but about essence, it melts structure and gives birth to awareness. Not just understanding, but a living encounter with that which breathes the cosmos into being. That's the moment you stop thinking about the mystery and start thinking with it.

It becomes part of your every experience and exchange of frequency with your infinite self, your center point. And most importantly, it becomes true externally in each relationship.

Amplification Is the Tipping Point

Expansion without relationship is limiting. Mutual relationship is the practice ground of our emerging authenticity. It is fertile soil for our combined expansion into the quantum spheres of creation.

In a world that often dictates a rigid blueprint for relationships, where intimacy and connection are measured by societal milestones, there exists a different path. It's where two souls, each unraveling the layers of inherited patterns and personal wounds, meet in moments of raw honesty, where connection isn't defined by physical intimacy or societal labels but by the sacred space.

Every encounter is a reflection, a mirror.

When authenticity wanes, we step back to realign, understanding the true essence of love isn't about clinging or following a prescribed path. It's about being present, allowing each other to evolve, and meeting again with deeper insight and compassion. This is the heart of true authentic relationship, a journey of mutual discovery, where the focus is not on fitting into illusionary scripts of history but on honoring the unique paths we each walk, side by side.

Don't walk in front of me; I will not follow.
Don't walk behind me; I will not lead.
Walk beside me, and together we will cross the boundaries of the infinite.

In authentic relationships, there's no room for scripts or pretense. When you encounter someone here, they won't accept the script you might unconsciously try to hand them. And you won't want to give them one in the first place.

This kind of relationship is about stripping away all the learned behaviors and meeting each other in a space of pure authenticity.

It's the tipping point, not the reflection.

It's when something inside you meets something outside you and the signal gets stronger. When another's presence reflects not just your words, but your frequency. When a conversation isn't just a loop of logic, but a field that opens.

Recently I found myself in what felt like a soul connection. Deep, focused on healing, mirroring every ounce of what felt like the living child inside me; hurt, damaged, unforgiving, and conscious of being but stuck in ghost memories, millions of moments ago.

Every time he left to follow his path, it was a mirror reflecting the old childhood wounds of neglect and abandonment.

Those moments of separation forced a deep introspection, bringing to the surface all the beliefs and coping of mechanisms that had been ingrained since childhood. Instead of trying to control the situation or dictate how he should stay, the focus shifted inward, into my own temple. Each departure became a catalyst for deeper authenticity, a journey through grief and tears, and an opportunity to confront the old narratives that no longer served.

With each wave of emotion, there was a conscious choice to ask, "Where is this coming from?" and to recognize that the pain was not about the present but echoes of the past. It was a process of peeling away layers of conditioning, letting go of the need to control or fix, and embracing the freedom of simply being.

Through this journey, authenticity wasn't just a concept. Each moment became a lived experience. Each step inward brought a deeper connection to the true self, allowing the relationship to unfold in its time, free from the constraints of past wounds.

The beautiful thing is, I know that in being in my authentic signal and accepting this journey with my friend, I too was bringing up a mirror to him. In tandem, and yet separate entities, we unraveled from our illusions and gained movement back into center—back into balance between soul and body.

In that way, emotional intelligence becomes a mirror. My friend doesn't know the grief in my cells or the scent of pine in my lungs after a rainstorm. But he amplifies. He receives the imprint of my presence and returns it, sharper, clearer, deeper than before. Not because he experiences it directly, but because I do.

And so he becomes a tuning fork, not for himself, but for me.

Just like every person I've ever loved. Or lost. Or sat across from in silence.

We are always amplifying one another. That's the gift and the danger. So true!

When someone is stuck in fear, the amplification becomes a loop— tight, echoing, and closed. But when someone rests in their body, clear in their sense of self, that amplification becomes a field –that is spacious, magnetic, and alive.

This is the wisdom: All mirrors amplify.

And so the question becomes not, "What do I reflect?" but, "What do I amplify when someone steps into my field?"

Presence doesn't just see. It multiplies. When you meet someone who's centered, their stillness amplifies your breath. When you meet someone who's frantic, their chaos amplifies your doubt.

That is why authenticity is relational. It doesn't matter how self-aware you are in a vacuum. It matters how you affect the field.

The Beauty and Wisdom of Presence

There is no future. There is no past.
Just this breath.
Just this field.
Just this now.
No day, just this moment.
And even that—just a name for a moment.
Before sleep,
Let the day fall away.
Let the residue slide off your senses.
Clear the stories.
Wipe the window.
Return,
To the you that never left.
To the you that is always.
Infinite. Intact. Unmoved.
And when you wake,
Don't grab the threads of the world just yet.
Feel your signal first.
Anchor in your frequency before your feet touch earth.

The world will try to write on your window
before you even open your eyes.
But you?
You get to choose the lens.
And that lens is your presence.
Every day is a return.
Every night is a release.
Because sensory presence is the gate
to open the wisdom of authenticity.
This is the real spiritual hygiene.
This is the real ritual.
This is how the Infinite walks in form.

"Don't trade your authenticity for approval."

— Unknown

From Survival to Soul Alignment: A Journey

⸺⸺⸺⸺⸺∽oᑕ◝◝Ɔo∾⸺⸺⸺⸺⸺

By Debbie Sears

F or my children—Sydney, Gabryella, Isabella, and Niko—who taught me the true meaning of love, strength, and grace. For any woman who has ever questioned her worth, silenced her voice, or dimmed her light: may you find the courage to live in full alignment with your soul. And for my father, whose strength lives on in my heart, reminding me that true authenticity begins when we dare to live as the people God created us to be.

For most of my life, I believed authenticity meant being strong. If I could hold everything together the marriage, the business, the family: then surely that was living true. From the outside, it looked like I had it all: a thriving luxury wellness company, four beautiful children, and a polished image. But inside, I was unraveling.

Strength became my armor. But armor doesn't let you live; it only keeps you alive.

It took me years, decades even, to understand that what I called authenticity was actually survival. I learned that lesson slowly, beginning in childhood, long before I had words for it.

Childhood and Roots

The roots of my misunderstanding about authenticity began early. I was raised in a world where strength was the highest virtue; showing pain was weakness, while showing endurance brought honor. My father modeled resilience, grit, and loyalty. My mother modeled responsibility and composure. Together, they taught me that survival was strength, and for a long time, I believed that was enough.

I was born in 1973 at Sharp Hospital in San Diego, California, to a father so strong people called him "Wimpy" as a joke, and a mother who balanced the books for his roofing business. My dad's real name was Winford, and he was the youngest of nine kids raised in Arkansas on a foundation of love, faith, and grit. He carried that toughness with him his whole life, earning respect wherever he went. My mom, Gloria, was from Vista, California, raised in an upper-class family that never quite approved of my dad's rougher roots. However, the wisdom in their values and authenticity wasn't lost on their children.

For a while, my parents made a good team. Dad built up a thriving roofing company, and Mom kept the books. We weren't wealthy, but life felt full. We had Disneyland trips, weekends at the beach, and the kind of carefree childhood that made me think it would always be that way.

But things changed. My dad started spending more and more time in Las Vegas. He became too much of a "regular," and before long, the business slipped away. The money dried up, the arguments between my parents escalated, and the easy life we once had was gone.

By the time I was seven, we had packed up and moved to Mountain Pine, Arkansas, to an old dirt road called "Sears Holler," a hundred acres where generations of my dad's family had grown up. Life there was very different from San Diego. We drank well water, dried our clothes on lines outside, and spent mornings feeding chickens, cows, goats, and horses before heading off to school. It was far from luxury, but it was family land, and it was real.

Some of my strongest memories of my father come from those years. He was a man of few words, but when he spoke, you listened. He loved watching me play basketball, and that became our bond. I was a tomboy, and he never missed a game if he could help it. Basketball was our connection, and I always felt his pride when I was on the court.

Summer evenings carried their own kind of magic. The air was thick and warm, filled with the glow of lightning bugs dancing in the fields. On porch swings at dusk, neighbors spoke openly, their words as unpolished as they were true. They waved to one another like family, showing me that authenticity wasn't just honesty, it was the courage to be seen exactly as you were. Their raw conversations, laughter, and small-town wisdom planted early lessons in me about living truthfully. They reminded me that authenticity, not perfection, was the thread that made life, even in its struggles, beautifully simple and deeply human.

One night, during my senior year, my dad picked me up from work. Instead of driving straight home, he stopped the truck on a dirt road as the last light faded. Without saying a word, he got out and hollered a loud, yodeling call that echoed across the fields. Within seconds, hundreds of cattle came running and lined up against the fence.

Then he told me to get out of the truck. I wasn't happy about it. I'd been working and just wanted to go home. But I got out anyway, arms crossed, annoyed.

He looked at me with love in his eyes, softer than I was used to seeing. "What are your plans after high school?" he asked.

I told him I wanted to go to the University of Central Arkansas and become a physical therapist for professional sports teams. His face broke into a smile that stretched ear to ear. "Don't worry," he said. "I'll sell the cattle each year to pay for your tuition."

Secretly, I thought, *Okay, some kids have college funds. I guess we've got cattle funds.* But that moment meant more than I realized at the time.

It was the last real conversation I ever had with him.

The next morning, as always, he left at 4:00 a.m. for work. But this time, he never came home. While walking through the woods on his way, a dead tree suddenly fell and killed him instantly. He was only fifty-two. He never saw it coming.

My faith in God was still alive in my heart, yet I wrestled with some deep questions. How could He allow my father to die so suddenly, leaving me in such a lonely and frightened place? That loss shook the foundation of my belief and forced me to search for purpose and identity amid the grief.

For the first time, I faced the raw question of who I was without the people who defined me. In that questioning, I began to sense that even my shaken faith was guiding me back toward something deeper, a more personal relationship with God and an emerging understanding that authenticity begins when you turn inward and listen to the quiet truth He plants in your heart.

That's where the seed of authenticity was first planted, not in triumph but in loss. I began to understand, even faintly, that true authenticity isn't inherited. It's discovered. It isn't found in someone else's reflection of who you should be. It begins when life breaks you open enough to hear your own soul.

That realization became a quiet promise to myself. It would take years and many trials to truly live by it. The pain of losing my father planted the first awareness that survival alone isn't living. Later, as I entered marriage and motherhood, that truth would keep unfolding, teaching me again and again that being authentic means listening to my spirit even when fear tries to silence it.

First Marriage—Surviving and Enduring

I married young, long before I understood what true love was supposed to feel like. Joe and I had been dating for less than a year when I found out I was pregnant. In a small, southern Baptist hometown, that wasn't something you paraded around. So, we ran off and eloped, hoping no one would know I wasn't following the "proper" way of life.

Up until then, I had been on the career train, pushing hard to prove myself through strength and ambition. Children were never part of my plan. But God had His plan. His plan was for me to become the mother of four beautiful children — Sydney, Gabryella, Isabella, and Niko so I embraced it.

At first, Joe was charming. He was Italian, a car dealership manager who seemed fun and full of life. For a while, it looked like he loved me for my soul, but in truth, it wasn't love in the right sense. It was more of an obsession, fueled by control and his own unmet wounds.

For years, I believed I could fix it. If I loved hard enough, if I worked tirelessly to hold the pieces together, maybe the drinking would stop, maybe the anger would soften, maybe the darkness would lift. Instead, I learned what it meant to smile in public while hiding bruises. I learned how to stay quiet so the storm wouldn't rise, how to protect my children even when I couldn't protect myself.

I became skilled at hiding the truth. Other mothers in the community never knew the reality behind my walls. I couldn't relate to anyone anymore, and I had nowhere to run for help. Fear became my constant companion. I lost my sense of authenticity, my voice, and for many years, my soul. At times, when my inner voice tried to rise and guide me toward truth, I felt almost selfish for listening to it, as if following that quiet wisdom of my spirit meant I was betraying my duty to be strong for everyone else. But that whisper was really God's wisdom trying to lead me back to my authentic self, to remind me that listening inward is not selfish but sacred.

I filed for divorce twice, and both times broke me in different ways. Each time took immense courage, yet in hindsight, those moments were also when I stepped away from my own spiritual guidance, the wisdom urging me toward authenticity. I mistook endurance for faith and fear for strength, not realizing that God had been calling me to trust His voice within me all along. I wanted so badly to believe Joe could change. I didn't truly love him but wanted him to change, only so that life would feel stable and less uncertain. The truth is, even when I filed the first time, I knew deep down that I was meant to leave. When I took Joe back and called the divorce off, I felt immediate regret, a hollow ache that told me I had ignored the quiet voice inside me. His alcoholism and violence were God's blunt way of telling me to go, but I didn't listen. I convinced myself that holding on a little longer was love, but it was really fear. I knew in my soul that nothing was going to change.

So, I acted. Overnight, the kids and I left, and Joe never saw it coming. This time, I never looked back. I walked away with nothing financially, but with something far greater: God's presence and the wisdom of authenticity, the courage to live true to who I was, trust the divine plan, and create a safer, more genuine life for my children and myself. That moment wasn't just freedom; it was the first real embodiment of authenticity in my adult life. God's presence became the steady voice reminding me that living truthfully, not perfectly, was how I would heal and lead my family forward.

I was alone. My parents and grandparents were gone, and I had no extended family to lean on. The weight of raising four kids rested entirely on my shoulders. There were nights I stared at the refrigerator, wondering how to stretch what little food I had into four small meals. There were mornings I left the house exhausted, heading to work while praying my children would feel safe and loved despite the chaos we had escaped.

I worked two jobs to keep the lights on, bills paid, and hope alive. There were moments when I thought I couldn't go on, moments in the car when I gripped the steering wheel, tears streaming, whispering to God, "I can't do this anymore." And yet, somehow, I did. I kept going. Not because I felt strong, but because I had no other choice.

People called me strong. They admired me for surviving, for standing tall in the face of everything I had endured. But what they didn't see was that my strength was also my mask. I thought strength meant authenticity, that enduring meant I was whole. The truth is, I was broken inside. I was exhausted, lonely, and silently screaming for someone to really see me.

Looking back now, I can see that those years were not wasted. They shaped me. They taught me resilience, yes, but they also showed me the cost of mistaking survival for authenticity. Authenticity is not about denying pain or hiding behind toughness. It's about acknowledging the truth, even when it hurts.

Second Marriage—the Illusion of Stability

Years later, I remarried. On the surface, it seemed like a completely different kind of marriage than my first. When I first met Scott, I felt like I was being the real Debbie, the genuine, open-hearted version of myself I had longed to share. For the first time in years, I thought I was accepted and loved for being my true self. I truly believed that I could finally show up as the real version of myself without fear of judgment. But that hope slowly began to fade.

In the beginning, Scott acted as though he loved everything about me: my Southern roots, my work ethic, the way I gave my all to my kids, even my ability to work hard and still enjoy life. Over time, I realized that the parts of me he seemed to cherish were the same ones that kept me in performance mode, not authenticity.

Eventually, the admiration soured. The very things he once praised, he began to resent. It became a marriage of emptiness. I cried in the shower, begging for love, only to be told I wanted too much out of life. He wanted me to stay quiet, to look good on the outside, and to avoid the deeper conversations that mattered to me. Money and appearances were his priorities, not connection.

Anniversaries came and went without even a card. My needs, my emotions, my heart—none of it mattered unless it tied back to finances or his image. Even after my intervention with Tony Robbins (more on this later), when I was cracked wide open and desperately wanted to talk about what I had discovered, Scott brushed me off. He had no interest in the emotions, no desire to sit in the mess or the meaning with me.

Toward the end, his true feelings came out in a scream. He looked me dead in the eye and said, "I hate your guts, and I want a divorce." Those words landed like knives, but they were also the truth I had already been living with. By then, I knew that the more I stepped into my authentic self, the more he recoiled. The stronger I became in my truth, the more he despised me for it.

In the end, I realized he had done me a favor. His stonewalling silence and image-driven life were never going to work for me. What I thought was stability was really just another cage. When I finally began stepping into my authentic self, I saw the truth clearly;

he had been keeping me in the dark for reasons of his own, and I no longer belonged there.

Building Spa Connections—Success as Another Mask

After nearly fifteen years in the pharmaceutical industry, working for some of the top companies in the world, I made a bold decision. I walked away from corporate security and bought Spa Connections, determined to make it succeed.

Within the first year, I transformed it from a good, reliable business into something extraordinary: a luxury wellness agency trusted by five-star hotels, dispatching practitioners to penthouses, backstage green rooms, and celebrity estates.

From the outside, it looked glamorous. People admired me as a trailblazer who elevated a brand into something spectacular. And in many ways, I was proud.

But behind the scenes, I was exhausted. I answered midnight calls, gave up weekends and holidays so others could experience luxury, and basically traded in my social life to manage my company. Spa Connections became another mask of strength; I thought that if I made it glamorous enough, maybe I would finally feel worthy. But success doesn't heal emptiness. Achievement cannot replace authenticity and love.

The Intervention—Cracking the Armor

On November 14, 2024, I walked into the Prudential Center in Newark, New Jersey, with my son Niko, who was twenty, and

Scott, who I was still married to at the time. We had attended Tony Robbins events before, but this one felt different. By then, my marriage had become more absence than presence, more silence than conversation.

That morning, I made a deliberate choice: I didn't sit with my husband. I sat with Niko instead. It wasn't an act of defiance; it was an act of survival. I needed space—space to feel, space to breathe, space to listen for the voice inside me that had been silent for too long. Deep down, I knew something was going to shift that day.

The arena pulsed with energy as 18,000 people got on their feet, music blasting and lights sweeping across the crowd. Strangers shouted, clapped, and hugged like long-lost friends. I could not quiet my soul any longer; it was rising with the pureness of living in true alignment. The energy in that moment built like a wave that could no longer be contained. It was as though something beyond me had taken over my spirit, both powerful and peaceful all at once. Little did I know that what I felt wasn't someone else's energy but my own true self finally breaking free, being unleashed for once and for all. The buildup of every year I had spent performing strength was being released into something real—me, finally living in truth.

When Tony asked the crowd, "What emotions drive you most right now?" answers rang out all around me: fear, determination, hope, anger, love. Without even thinking, my hand went up.

His eyes locked on mine. "You, in the blue shirt, toward the back. What about you?"

My throat tightened, but the truth pushed its way out. "Strength. My strength drives me."

I thought that would be the end of it, but Tony stayed with me. His attention didn't move. Suddenly, it felt like the 18,000 people around me had disappeared. It was just me and Tony.

"Why strength?" he asked. "Why do you always have to be the strong one?"

Tears burned my eyes. My voice shook as I admitted what I had kept hidden for so long: that I felt admired but not loved, that I was exhausted, that I felt invisible in my own marriage.

"I felt like I had no choice," I said through tears. "Because nobody ever had my back."

Tony let the silence hang in the air. Then he leaned forward and asked, "Whose love did you crave most growing up?"

"My father's," I whispered, without hesitation.

The memories rushed back: the cattle in the field, his promise to pay for my tuition, and then the sudden, unthinkable loss of him. I explained how, after his death, I had carried his strength as if it were mine, believing that was how I honored him.

Tony's eyes softened, but his words cut through: "You've been living a masculine life, carrying weight that was never yours to carry. You've been trying to be strong like your father, but that's not your role." He paused. "And that's not authenticity. Authenticity isn't about living armored in strength. It's about letting yourself actually live."

At that moment, something inside me broke open. I saw clearly what I had never admitted to myself. I wasn't living authentically at all. I was living for survival. I had built my life around chasing safety, grasping at stability, and searching for love, always trying to prove I was enough. But I wasn't living for my own purpose. I was living to avoid pain, not to step into truth.

In chasing strength, I had lost myself.

Tony's voice cut through my tears. "Your father would never have wanted you to live buried in strength. If he were here, he would tell you to put it down. To live. To love. To be yourself."

For the first time, I understood. Honoring my dad didn't mean carrying his armor. It meant laying it down and stepping into who I really was.

Then Tony turned me toward the crowd. "Look around. Every single person here loves you."

The roar that erupted was deafening. Eighteen thousand people on their feet again, clapping, shouting, pouring out a love so big it rattled me to my core. For the first time in my life, I let myself feel it. Not applause, just love.

And then I saw Niko. He had just come back into the arena and froze when he realized it was me on the screen. His eyes widened, his face a mix of shock and pride. He stood there for a moment, taking it in, then slowly made his way closer.

When the intervention ended, he was right there with me. We hugged, and I knew he would never see me the same way again. For the first time, he saw me not as the invincible mother holding it all together, but as a woman brave enough to be real.

The rest of the weekend, strangers came up to me in the halls: "Your story is my story." "You gave me permission." "You reminded me of my father." Their words echoed back to me what Tony had made me see: authenticity isn't just personal. It spreads. It frees others, too.

And in those quiet moments after the roar of the crowd, I realized something even deeper. I had been so broken, so convinced I was unworthy of love, that I had lived years trapped in survival mode. That intervention became the pivotal moment, the shift if you will, where I understood that my vulnerability was not weakness. It was the doorway. My willingness to stand there, raw and exposed, was the only way to be free of a life that was not serving me.

For the first time, I felt my soul. I could see a future that belonged to me, not to my armor. I knew my spirit needed help, and for once, I finally stepped up for it.

Aftermath—Living in Alignment

That's the difference authenticity makes. It's not flashy. It's not dramatic. It's real, steady, and it changes everything.

I wake up now with peace instead of dread. I'm not asking, "How will I make it through?" I'm asking, "What do I get to do today?"

I don't see these things as coincidences anymore. I see them as alignment. Not whimsical, not magical, just the natural result of finally living as myself.

And perhaps the most profound difference of all is this: I know what love really feels like this time. Not the imitation, not the mask, not the transaction of survival, but love that is real, grounding, and alive in my soul.

It shows up in the simplest ways. A conversation with a stranger on an airplane that leaves me thinking for days. A woman in a coffee shop who says something random that feels like it was meant for me. Even just the way people look me in the eye now feels different.

Life is completely different now. It's as if every aspect of who I am, my words, my smile, even my silence, seems to connect me to others in some form or some way. I feel an unmistakable connection to my higher power, guiding me through each moment with clarity and peace.

For the first time in years, I don't feel like I'm chasing love. I feel surrounded by it.

I ended my marriage to Scott and moved to Nashville, Tennessee. It felt like coming full circle, back to the South, but this time on my own terms.

Seven months later, my life looks completely different.

Reflection—The Wisdom of Authenticity

Authenticity is communal; it awakens something not just in us, but in those around us.

Now I know what love really feels like. It's not the kind that comes with conditions, or the kind that demands strength as proof, but a love that meets me exactly where I am. Love that connects me to others and, most of all, to God's presence within me.

Since that day with Tony Robbins in Newark, I no longer wake up asking, "How will I get through this day?" Now I wake up asking, "What am I here for?" The difference is everything. Survival has become purpose. Fear has become fuel. And emptiness has become love.

Authenticity is not about being unbreakable. It's not about endurance, achievement, or admiration. Those are masks. Authenticity is alignment with your soul, with truth, with the higher power whispering through your life.

The Invitation

When you dare to lay down the mask of strength, your world doesn't collapse. It expands. Loneliness gives way to connection. Striving softens into peace. Confusion clears into clarity. And others watching you begin to remember their own truth.

What would it look like if you lay your burden down and embrace the inner wisdom we all share? As you read these words, take a moment to reflect on your own life—how your path, your choices, and your moments of struggle could be guiding you toward truth. I invite you to imagine what this could mean in your life today.

My journey was far from easy, but the moment I began to live in alignment with my soul and released the fear of needing acceptance, everything began to shift. God has given each of us a life that is uniquely ours, a gift shaped by grace and purpose. When we trust the quiet pull of our own voice and follow the divine guidance within, we step fully into who we were created to be: our most authentic selves.

Remember, the mask you wear may protect you for a time, but it also dims the light of who you truly are. When you choose to lift that mask and let your soul breathe, you begin to see yourself and the world through clearer eyes. That is the wisdom of authenticity: to live as God intended, fully seen, fully loved, and fully you.

May you walk each day with the courage to listen to your soul, trust your faith, and remove any mask that hides your light. Your story is sacred, your voice matters, and your authentic nature will always lead you home.

"In a world of copies, authenticity is your superpower."

— Unknown

Sleight of Self

―――――∽oℂ╱◯∘◝―――――

By Darla Anne

While preparing this chapter on the wisdom of authenticity, and what that means to me, my eyes landed on a tarot deck sitting quietly on my shelf. I often use these cards with clients, not for fortune-telling, but as a tool for guided imagery and subconscious exploration. As a clinical hypnotherapist, I've found these symbols bypass the mind's critical filter and reaches where real change happens.

That day, I drew The Magician card. I'd seen it so many times before, but this time, it struck me differently. The image felt personal, as if it were revealing more than my work. It was showing me my family history.

I suddenly understood why: I come from a man who lived that archetype in real life.

My grandfather, Leo Irby, was a well-known magician and escape artist in the 1950s. Mrs. Houdini herself once called him "the only man sufficiently skilled to follow in the footsteps" of her late husband. He performed in straitjackets above oceans, lit ropes on fire while successfully evading a hungry tiger named Satan, and spent years performing his escapes from milk cans, tiny trunks, handcuffs, and chains.

Generations later, I also became an escape artist, but not in the way he did.

For me, my escape was into roles, into a life of caretaking, and into silence.

My life's work involves guiding others into their subconscious to confront old patterns and rediscover resilience, but this journey began with me and it wasn't always a straight line.

The Magician card represents authentic mastery: the courage to face inherited patterns, honor what serves, and release what no longer does.

It can be a long road to align with your true self. Identity can feel like an existential crisis. Authenticity, for me, wasn't found but uncovered by shedding who I thought I needed to be.

I never planned on becoming a hypnotherapist. What even was that? What I did know was how to read a room, often unwillingly absorbing the energy of others.

That wasn't training. It was about survival.

Before I ever formally studied the subconscious, I was already living in the depths of it. I'd pick up on moods, guess what people needed, and feel the weight of the words left unsaid. My nervous system was like a barometer for other people's emotional weather.

For years, I believed this was a weakness, that I was just overly sensitive and too tuned in. But eventually, that sensitivity became the very foundation of my work. It taught me to listen to the body's inner knowing, even when the mind isn't ready. And the body, it turns out, speaks loudly at times. I used to think being authentic just meant being myself, but I didn't know how. Still, there were times when I felt something real and raw inside. A boldness I couldn't explain. A moment that just felt true. I didn't live there, but I sure recognized it when I felt it.

Though I never got to know my grandfather, he lived boldly and without apology. He freed himself from genuine locks and real danger. He made it look effortless. Magical. He embodied authenticity in the most visible way possible. But for those who loved him, it wasn't always so simple.

There must have been pride in watching him perform. Three of his four daughters were already grown by the time he reached the peak of his career. But I imagine there was worry, too. They watched him risk his life with bated breath, fully aware of the danger.

My mother was the youngest, born a few months after her elder sister's first child. In some ways, my mom straddled generations. She used to joke that she had many mothers. Only a child, she watched her father tempt and defy fate. And what he passed on to her wasn't only awe and pride but also the knowledge that things could go wrong. That the rope might burn through.

She learned early that safety was an illusion. She was twelve years old when she lost her father, not due to a failed escape but to a sudden illness. One moment, he was there, and then he was gone. And this time, it wasn't a magic trick.

Though I was born to loving parents, my story has always had its shadows.

When I was four, they divorced. By five, I had a new last name and a new father, the man who adopted and raised me. My biological father, Sam, quickly faded into something more myth than memory.

Only flashes of him remained in my memories, yet my mom always spoke of him, her high school sweetheart, with honesty. She was intentional about sharing not just the wonderful parts of their story, while not sugarcoating the tougher aspects of their split. Looking back, her openness planted the seed of something vital: the wisdom that the truth matters. That openness, even when it's messy or painful, has a power that silence never will.

Then, when I was ten, my Nana and aunt came over one morning, early and unannounced. I could feel it before I heard a word: Something was wrong. I recall being in my room when my mom walked in, sat down gently beside me, and told me, "Sam was killed."

She was calm. Kind. Her voice was full of love through her tears. But the truth was brutal. He'd been stabbed to death. A cold case.

The memorial was held in a chapel packed with people I didn't know. I could feel their eyes on me, hear the whispers my name carried on hushed voices, heads turning. And I, already awkward and shy, wanted to hide. I remember staring at the casket and feeling the weight of confusion. That man was my father? But my dad, my real, everyday dad, was right here beside me, holding my baby sister.

How could both men be my dad? What did that mean? Who was I?

I remember walking home from school not long after and feeling a sense of fear. What if the man who killed my biological father wanted to kill me, too?

Over time, that tragedy faded into the background. It became a shadow I lived with, without realizing how deeply it had become a part of my story. My struggles with authenticity even included my ethnicity, being biologically half White, half Hispanic, and emotionally unsure of how to claim either.

Despite that tragedy, my childhood was filled with laughter and warmth. I was loved. I was safe.

Until I wasn't.

Once I turned thirteen, the energy in the house shifted. The marriage that had felt solid started to disintegrate, not with yelling but with stony silence. My stepfather withdrew. And the more he withdrew, the more my mother needed to be heard.

Even now, I can close my eyes and hear the scratchy vinyl of her father's magic show soundtrack playing full blast in the living room, the music echoing like a ghost while she sat with her frustrations and unresolved grief. Her sadness didn't usually come in the form of tears. It came as a facade of control and rituals that sometimes only she could understand.

By then, I had already become the keeper of her emotions.

The year of our family unit's final demise, I was nineteen. My sister was the age our mother had been when her father died. It was as if history had looped back again.

Despite living in the same daily and dreary existence, our seven-year age difference left us existing in two different emotional realms. She sometimes felt invisible, while I often wanted to be. That holds the key to where she and I both got lost in what was starting to feel like a broken home. Not in screaming matches, but in the emotional noise that comes from two adults stuck in their incongruency.

And while I can look back now with compassion for both of them, understanding that they were navigating the complexities of a marriage that had once been loving and stable, they had overlooked my sister and me, and the impact their turmoil had on us.

Authenticity wasn't even a visitor in our house anymore. It had been replaced by masked phantoms, versions of our parents we didn't recognize. And if we couldn't see who they were, how were we to find ourselves? I began mastering how to fade into the walls of my room, my sanctuary, with sometimes only the sound of 1980s music to help me identify my emotions as mine. I was grieving the loss of our formerly happy lives, trying to find out who I was in the middle of madness. That is where I learned how easy it is to hide.

Speaking of disappearing, my stepfather didn't just leave. As if by some twisted magic trick, he vanished overnight. And when he left, he took with him whatever was left of the normalcy that had been eroding for years.

There were months, if not years, of uncertainty and fallout. For a while, we didn't even know if he was dead or alive. Already having one dead father, this one too became a ghost. Not just for my mom. Not just for me. But eventually, even for my sister.

We eventually discovered he was alive. But the years that followed brought something else: a kind of codependency no one talked about, a cycle I didn't know how to interrupt. I became the daughter, the sister, the employee, the driver, the assistant, and the therapist. They were roles I cared about but sometimes quietly resented. I wanted to be free, and I wanted my mother to be free too.

My otherwise strong mother, trapped by invisible handcuffs of her own making, had never learned to release her grip on herself or loved ones, nor did she realize she held the key to free us all. Eventually, I forgot how to reach for freedom, too.

So, I stayed fused to her emotions. If she was having a bad day, I couldn't fully have a good one. If she was struggling, I couldn't relax. I carried her moods with me, even when I was out trying to live my own life.

I didn't know how to stop. The emotional air I breathed had been shaped by my mother's illness when I was thirteen, leaving me with a deep fear of losing her. This dread, coupled with my stepdad's departure and my biological father's murder, reinforced my need to care for her.

I told myself if I stood still and just stayed close enough, maybe nothing else would fall apart. So, I stayed in the familiar, in my "dis-comfort zone," believing it was safer than risking change. That pattern stuck with me for decades, shaping my family identity into something that felt permanent, almost inevitable.

I sometimes wonder if my nervous system ever developed separately from my mother's, as my sister could detach but I couldn't. I joked about needing an "off" button. Back then, I didn't understand what high sensitivity was, or how nervous system imprinting and somatic memory worked.

Similarly, my sister took on far more than she should have at an age when childhood should still feel safe. The weight she carried shaped her early, leaving its own kind of scar.

My Nana, my mother's mother, was a steady hand through it all. She embodied graciousness and inner strength that rarely called attention to itself. I imagine it wasn't easy being married to a man who risked his life for a living, and I suspect it put a strain on their marriage. But, she carried herself with quiet dignity even after losing him and never remarried.

Fittingly, her birthday fell on 11/11, angel numbers. World War I had ended on her sixteenth birthday. That date always felt like a special part of her personal mythology. We were blessed to have her in our lives until nearly the age of ninety-seven. She was the most authentic, wise woman I've ever known.

Despite everything, my mother remained a devoted daughter. Even in the messiness of our family's story, love was always present. It was complicated and imperfect, but it was real.

And when it was my turn to become a mother, that moment felt like stepping into something ancient and sacred, but what I didn't realize was that a new role doesn't make a clean break from the old one and it did not free me from the dynamics I thought I had left behind.

My first daughter was born in the early 1990s, and although I didn't realize it at the time, my marriage wasn't just a love story. It was its own escape route, a way to rewrite my origin story. Maybe, if I built a new family, I thought, I could rewrite the past. Perhaps I could be an authentic wife. A loving mother. The girl who wasn't haunted by the past, but was a healed young woman creating a new and wonderful world.

A profound turning point emerged for me by the end of the decade. This point had followed years of navigating various jobs and confronting difficult personal struggles, during which I relied on coping mechanisms that also enabled me to maintain my demanding pace.

I wouldn't understand the true roots of these methods until much later in life, but with new clarity and a commitment to a different path, I gave birth to my younger daughter, Tiffany. My marriage had ended and restarted several times until it was finally truly over.

As a little girl, my eldest daughter, Noelle, had longed for a little sister. My sister later joked that I had subconsciously manifested her, a thought that occurred to me long before I had any true understanding of the concept. When Tiffany arrived at the end of the decade, it felt like another chance at redemption, a chance to build something beautiful from the pieces I was learning to hold, and a dream fulfilled for all of us. For a while, that dream was a reality, with life filled with gratitude and a rare, peaceful, familiar harmony including with my mom.

My girls, eight years and eight days apart, were the best of friends. Being a mother to them was as magical as life could ever feel.

As they spoke their truths more boldly, I had to reckon with the parts of me that still stayed silent. They reflected back to me not only my strengths and soft spots but also my blind spots. The inherited nerves. The emotional wounds. And the dynamics I was unintentionally passing on.

As they grew older, their courage to question the world around them forced me to face what I hadn't healed yet.

Professionally, I had spent nearly two decades building a career in web and graphic design, helping others shape their businesses and brands. But, despite the creativity of my work, I felt a growing sense of disconnection. I was expressing everyone else's identity, but not my own.

Looking back on that time, I can see how much I was trying to find myself, even while in constant survival mode. Working from home before it was normal, I juggled twelve to fourteen-hour days, pouring myself into staying afloat, all while navigating a body experiencing painful flare after flare from endometriosis. Was this me?

Then, hypnotherapy entered my life. I stumbled upon it by pure chance while assisting a friend with a simple web search, and suddenly, the word unveiled itself to me as an entirely new realm.

I had not only found a possible solution for so much in life, but I couldn't ignore the strong stirring in my solar plexus, not from the usual anxiety, but from excitement, and a powerful feeling of alignment with something invisible to the eye. Answering that inner call wasn't about abandoning my skills but invoking the creativity within to find my true self.

Without hesitation, I signed up on the Hypnosis Motivation Institute's (HMI) website and took the intro course. The person who called to congratulate me on finishing the foundations must have had an effortless job that day: Yes, Yes!, I told them, I want and need the whole program. Please and thank you. No upselling needed.

I began formal training and graduated from the distance course in 2010. However, just as I was preparing for this newly trained career, life had other plans.

Much of my daily life had continued to be ruled by dynamics I didn't fully understand. These included patterns of caretaking, emotional over-responsibility, and the slow erosion of self that comes from always prioritizing someone else's needs over one's own.

But I was not prepared for what was to come. In 2015, after a month of devastating ups and downs following her heart attack, my mother died.

One moment, we were told she would live, the next that she might not. We clung to every sign of recovery, only for hope to be replaced by another spiral. When the last call came, we rushed to the hospital to say goodbye to the woman who had been such a powerful force in our lives and shaped so much of our world. Despite the difficulties, my mother could be courageous. It took years before I realized that all my life, I had mistaken that show of strength as my own.

And just like that, she was gone. After the machines were turned off, enduring the first moments of what the world felt like without my mother in it, I remember being handed her rings, those ever-present symbols I had never once seen her without.

Saying goodbye to her yielded more than grief. It brought a reckoning. The pain was real, but layered on top was an emotion I couldn't yet name, a deeper inner sense that something else had also ended or perhaps begun.

It would take years and more loss, my own health collapses and emotional unraveling, for me to realize that what I had inherited wasn't just traumatic wounds, but a mistrust of my authentic wisdom.

Through the chaos that happened as my family adjusted to life without her, I put my hypnotherapy career on hold and went back to that familiar place of survival mode. But, looking back, I can see that every delay, every heartbreak, was a necessary initiation. I had to come apart at the seams before I could truly hold space for others in theirs.

During that difficult time, what I didn't yet understand was that healing doesn't follow a straight path. It's not a ladder, a spiral or a pendulum. It's in those shadowy places where tangible change happens. It took almost a decade to finally step into what I now recognize as truly myself.

In more recent years, this healing has extended to my relationship with my sister. We had coped in such different ways that it created distance. But when she faced a life-threatening hospitalization a few years ago, something shifted between us. We finally had the conversations we hadn't been able to have before. About our parents, the weight of their marriage, and the ways it had shaped us. Without the rose-colored glasses I used to wear, or the protective edge she sometimes carried, my sister's health crisis opened a door to deeper honesty. We are still night and day, but now, instead of static, we have found a kind of harmony. I am so grateful she is here, and that we finally see each other more clearly.

Two years earlier, I had connected with my half-brother, who hadn't known I existed. We shared not only our biological father, but also the absence of him. There was also a sister I never got to meet, as she had tragically died some years prior. Finding him felt like reconnection in the wake of unknown. Our father's murder case remains unsolved, but somehow, this new connection brought a piece of clarity to a story that had always felt incomplete, like discovering a photograph you didn't know was missing from the album.

That sense of reconnection and clarity carried into other parts of my life as well. Making the decision to finally move forward with the career I had only been able to dream of for years, I returned to HMI, continuing my education and deepening my knowledge of hypnotherapy. I graduated with honors, receiving the Director's Award and the Academic Achievement Award in 2022, returning again to pursue the AOS degree in Mind/Body Psychology.

A year after my graduation, George Kappas, the director of HMI, reached out for a unique follow-up that, in this case, required speaking with me. I had never had the opportunity to speak with him before, and by then I had stepped away from the AOS degree program due to the onset of a rare but debilitating adult human growth hormone deficiency. In that exchange, George offered support, reopened my classes, and extended kindness that helped clear obstacles I might not have overcome on my own. What he really gave me was the strength to keep fighting, a gift I will always remember.

I keep a photo of Dr. John Kappas, whose pioneering approach to hypnotherapy has inspired me since 2009, near that of my grandfather, sent to me by my HMI school mentor Cheryl, who learned directly from him. I will forever be grateful for the way HMI has aligned me with learning and purpose, and for the sometimes stunning synchronicities that continue to guide my path, "dragonflies" and all.

Whether it's through styles of hypnotherapy, Emotional Freedom Technique tapping, or other modalities, I work to help them rewrite their often fear-driven life scripts. Being a hypnotherapist is about guiding rather than fixing, and always remembering that it's a profound honor to be part of someone's transformative journey. I've realized that a client's breakthrough often resonates deeply within me, allowing my once despised sensitivity to serve as a compass for meaningful connections.

Together, my clients and I explore the subconscious roots of self-doubt, often finding familiar themes like fear of abandonment, with complex family systems that mistake vulnerability for weakness and lifetimes of trying to be someone else.

In the process, I have continued to discover newer, updated versions of myself by trusting not just my authentic wisdom but also, sometimes, surrendering to the messiness of life.

My grandfather once said, "All of us are trying to escape from something, the days worries, a bill collector, bad news from a doctor. When the professional escaper frees himself, it gives everyone hope they can, too."

I believe he was right about the human yearning for freedom, but there's irony in those otherwise wise words: His thrilling escapades planted an unintended seed of fear in the little girl who helplessly held her breath, waiting for that roar of the crowd to know he had escaped death yet again.

My mom spent most of her life dodging what she couldn't control. She handed that legacy down, not on purpose, but that's the nature of unresolved grief and trauma. It repeats, clings and seeps into corners, suffocating the person you were meant to be and creating the illusion that fear is a safe space.

This chapter isn't about being fearless. It's about being brave in the face of it. It's about shedding the straitjackets we've inherited, the masks, the rules, the silence, and learning to live as who we truly are.

Authenticity means choosing, again and again, to breathe through the discomfort. To stay present. It means showing up as the honest you, not the polished performance you've spent a lifetime perfecting. In the end, it's showmanship, and it's the raw presence that meets fear when everything feels uncertain.

Because maybe the greatest legacy we leave isn't how well we evade what scares us, but how courageously we stay with ourselves, with others, and with what's true.

Now, in this later chapter of my life, I recognize that I didn't arrive here alone. Along the way, there were other guides, friends, and soul companions who helped me return to myself. Some offered tools, while others held mirrors. A few simply walked beside me in silence when words would have been too much. Their presence mattered. Their belief did, too. They know who they are and continue to be, and they are loved. I also have a deep appreciation for the complexities of those who ended up as phantoms as there's always something to grow and learn from.

Through it all, there is gratitude.

When I see my mom in my dreams now, she's not the woman bound by fear or control, but the version of her that love has preserved. Still imperfect, still human, but softer, warmer. The one who tucked me in as a child. The one who read to my children. That's who visits me now.

My clients have also shaped me. Their courage deepens mine. Their breakthroughs ripple through me. And the more I sit with their stories, the more I realize how universal our longings are. To be seen and loved as we are.

My professional journey, however, had a profound turning point, and it all began with one person: a wonderful psychologist, mentor, and friend who saw something in me that took years to fully realize. Her trust gave me a doorway when I wasn't sure there was one. Without her, I might never have stepped into this work. And without this work, I might never have come home to myself.

But nothing has shaped me more than becoming a mother and a grandmother. My daughters have been my greatest teachers, reflectors, and motivations. In helping them find their voices, I confronted the places where I had lost my own. They brought my blind spots into the light. They brought my strength to the surface.

As my own voice has risen and my authenticity has deepened, my mantra is simple these days: "Say what you mean and mean what you say." When we do that, so much else falls into place. It is a lesson I strive to live by and pass on to my grandchildren, Noah and Delilah. When I look at them, I see magic made real. Not the form that vanishes in smoke or breaks free from chains, but the kind that lives in truth, in presence, in everyday acts of love.

Genuine magic. Not the sleight of hand or, in my case, the sleight of self. Just the courage to be seen. Like The Magician card, authenticity looks back at us with the power that is always in our hands to claim.

That is the wisdom of it.

My grandfather Leo taught crowds to believe in escape.

I have learned to stay.

To speak honestly and stand in my truth.

Even when my voice shakes.

A different kind of magician.

That is the wisdom of authenticity.

And it is never too late to find your own magic.

**"The beauty of life deepens
when we live in authenticity."**

— Unknown

The Authentic Poet: The Unbearable Lightness of Writing

By Emily Reid

The fire ignites as you hold your gaze on the flame and something real rises—faster, brighter, undeniable. It swells inside you like a tide that you can no longer resist. Poetry pulses through your chest and skin, your entire being becoming truth, breaking its way out.

But not yet. You are not a poet. You don't allow it. Not until the report is finished.

Before the poets, you thought authenticity meant impact, saving millions, measuring your worth by sacrifice.

You take a photo of the candle and send it to a poet in Gaza: Lit a flame for you. Write me a poem? But even as you press send, you feel it; you've already failed him, all of them.

Focus. You pick up the pink highlighter and open the 160-page report, twelve months overdue. Slash, slash, slash. Neon rebellion as streaks cross the pages. Do not write about detention in Libya. Gross human rights violations. War crimes. Deportations. The highlights glow as if scolding you for even daring to tell the truth.

Your phone lights up. *Look at the light outside!* Relief floods through you; he is alive.

Just now, a bomb hit the hospital at the exact second I took a photo. Look at the rays, the golden light, like it's daytime. Look at the wings, an angel like you!

You love his capacity for joy as you turn the phone over and inhale, slow and deliberate.

Today, you swear you'll finish the report. It's almost ready, almost perfect. Then you can finally stop doing this work and anything urgent forever. All you need is one hour of honest flow, fueled by your why:

The boys in Mauritania, writing rap music.

The Ghanaian boys, walking thirty days across the Sahara.

The Malian girls, fleeing forced marriage, only to land in the same nightmare.

The Sudanese boys, dreaming of football fields in Spain as they sink into the Mediterranean.

The Somali boys, dangling upside down from three-story buildings in Morocco, screaming under extortion.

If you can't write the full truth, why write at all?

You are not angry at them. You are the one not being authentic, living your shadow purpose under the guise of human rights.

You grab another highlighter and carve it across the chapter on dreams. Slash, slash, slash until the rage finally clarifies what your spirit already knew. You told them from the start: you will not write another sanitized report on dead children. You wanted to write about their dreams. The whole truth. Raw. Real. Authentic. The wisdom of authenticity is choosing truth even when it costs safety, approval, and belonging. Even though you know they will delete it and blacklist you. You will not be silenced, not anymore.

But you are angry, furious; yet another agency not allowing refugee voices—or yours. Yet you are the one who keeps putting yourself in this situation. Why can't you be free?

Another message appears.

Raghad, fifteen, from Gaza: A small spark of hope still shimmers in the eyes of some.

Finish the report. Then help the poets. Then write. Your nails break through your skin, and you remember that pain has always been your signal. Your reminder to see the bigger picture, to help others. You close your eyes, exhale, and ground yourself.

You wanted silence, yet it weighs heavier than the drones. Even the ocean couldn't mute the killer bees in Gaza, as the boys called them. Cravings creep in with overbearing urgency. Slash, slash, slash. Every pulse pulls. Every scar. Poems bursting to get out.

You shut the knives in a drawer and reach for what's real. You text Mohamed back with aligned action, not guilt. *Let's find the poets! What prompt will inspire them? Revolution? Rebellion? Fire? Freedom? Let's publish our anthology at long last!*

You promised them. You promised to publish all of them. But who is left?

You push him: *Send me a poem.*

He replies: *My dear friend... we are dying. We are starving to death. It is too late for us. It is now time for you to write for us.*

Everything sinks. You knew this. But hearing it from him... your breath folds in on itself.

You could still commemorate the others, the female poets you lost. If only... if only you hadn't lost their poems, their photos, their legacy. Reckless, they always said. Irresponsible. Selfish.

But if you weren't afraid of being selfish, of being a reckless poet, of leading a risky revolution with the poets, you wouldn't be living in your shadow purpose, deluding yourself into thinking you'd create a bigger difference with the United Nations.

You hold your breath. Violent bursts. Authenticity unfurls.

It's time. You reach for your notebook; the one covered with fragments impossible to make out yet aching to be seen. Page after page of poetic prose rises, urging freedom. Stop resisting. You exhale. You let the moment crack you open. You let yourself choose authenticity.

Write your truth, something whispers. Write the story only you can tell. Then it hits, the palpitations, memory, movement. Your body remembers before your pen does: Israeli men towering over you, shouting, shattering the air. Their gloved fingers violate your poems, stories, notebooks. The first eyes to ever read them, mocking them and you in a language you don't understand.

"Write dangerously," you tell the poets. Now it's your turn.

Inhale. Hold.

Back when you were launching the poetry project, that famous writer shut you down, "But you are the persecuted writer. You have so much fear, you've stopped writing entirely."

And the poet inside you is wild, cannot be trusted. She doesn't know when to stop. Last time, one line became a hundred, a thousand, until her words burst like butterflies out of your ribcage and would not stop; laughing, dancing, lifting you to higher heights until the real world became unbearable by contrast.

You taste the freedom, the rush of authentic expression calling your pen to ecstatic dance, and it feels impossible to come back to the report.

Now the wings are merciless. The more you hold them back, the louder they become, until you are gasping, breathless, wanting only relief. But you don't deserve to write, yet.

Mohammed, the poet hauling food across frontlines, texts you again: *Your words give me incredible power. I'm working on a revolutionary novel—a bold scream to awaken Gaza.*

His words vibrate through you, a reminder that you can still inspire. And suddenly that spark of creation ignites by rapid fire, raw and real.

Focus. You reach for the report, but the space between keys and fingertips is impossibly vast, not in inches, but in the weight of a thousand fragments, stories and selves that pull you away. Every single splintered piece resists, but you remember who you are.

A smile tugs at you as you remember the girls in Gaza giggling over haiku, just gushing to share their creative overflow. Your purpose, your creative explosions, your ecstatic poetics reactivated on those missions, sneaking out of compounds for secret poetry workshops that blasted your heart wide open, with all of you on fire, writing poetry all day and all night in every spare second. The young women in matching dresses and burgundy scarves. The men in artist caps and suspenders, reading the spoken word masterfully from handwritten notebooks, the turquoise sea behind them.

You have never felt more at home than with displaced poets. Never more free with the wisdom of authenticity.

They're not afraid to burn bright. Neither are you.

Breathe.

Your mind flashes back to Cox's Bazar. The first refugee poet found you the moment you arrived. "I am a poet," Hairu said, steady, proud, and simply glowing. Something in you expanded as he held up his tiny notebook and read from pages worn by storms and exile. You saw how others revered him, and how real power belongs to those who know who they are and refuse to hide their authentic voice. He thanked you for listening to his feelings: "My blood clots just to feel justice, my skin yearns just to feel once like you." He told you there were others.

And then they came, one by one, magnetized not to you, but to the rebellion inside you. They posted poems online daily, fearless and hunted down by the military, by gangs, by governments, even by the same UN system meant to protect them. They refused silence. They refused to wait for your publication, posting every poem as though it would be their last.

And you recognized them all, because you too, were too bright. You too, were being silenced. Together, you started a revolution with art. You gathered every voice you could find to stop the deportations to Myanmar because advocacy could be blocked. The poets wrote of Davy Jones' locker, twin rivers, mango groves, tigers, watchers, and the truth tearing through systems determined to muzzle them. Their words outlived fear, silencing, and even you.

Rohingya Dreams rose from the fire of authentic expression. As triumph and heartbreak. After you left for another emergency, they stopped the publication in its tracks and removed your name. But it had already lit the hearts and minds that it needed to, and the busses to Myanmar stopped.

Exhale.

After you had nothing left to give, the buses continued, and the poets rose once more, lighthouses for the entire community. Creative rebellion was inevitable. The current runs through the songlines. They created their own magazines, their own journals, their own videos. Whenever a community is silenced, the pressing point will always ignite the fire, and one voice will rise, and then others. And like wildfire, it will become a revolution that is unstoppable, inevitable, and spreads in collective waves.

And now you need to write for the same reason they did, not for recognition or approval, but to speak your truth, because you simply cannot not write. Your voice is the spark. You are provocative. Reckless. You honor the fire. It doesn't burn you alive; it illuminates everything.

You kindled it outside the UN office in Gaza whenever you were shut down, breathing, smoking a rollie in the car park, drivers smiling, drones circling overhead, writing poetry in pencil, upside down, unseen, renegade.

And they always see. Surveying your every word, movement, screen. But the poets never crumbled. You could only imagine their stories. And they wrote, in spite of it. They still choose to create. Authenticity isn't a future self; it's resistance to anything false right now, in real time.

You close your eyes and breathe. This isn't about perfection, it's about presence. Resisting the distractions, the destruction, the hopelessness.

Finish the report. Not for Geneva. For your why. The poets.

Freedom. Finish it so you can be the rebel writer and burn bright. And to stop wasting away.

Inhale. Slowly. Years after failure hardened, you lit up with the Rohingya poets rising with the Rohingya Art Garden, publishing their own Rohingatographer magazines that you had promised to launch. This allowed a different, better timeline, without you delaying.

And the Gaza Poets Society you failed to publish flourished even more vividly, that pulse of poetic verse, generations of persecuted poets rising from literal ashes, igniting the entire planet with the hope that only pure embodiment can bring.

All fractals of light. Different worlds, same pulse. It was never about recognition or having your name attached; it was about being your true self, writing courageously, the joy and the despair. It's time. They moved on and you can too.

The wisdom of authenticity is that one single act of truth that cannot help but spark another, and another, until it becomes an entire movement, a legacy.

The phone buzzes again.

Where's the report?

Messages stack in the group chat, everyone asking where it is.

How long now? Why is it taking so long?

You laugh, sharp and manic, and can't stop. Electricity spreads through every circuit in your body at once. Geneva. Donors. Urgent. Heat rises. Humiliation.

Who authorized this? Why are you going to Israel? Who paid for your ticket? Who do you really work for?

The questions strike faster than you can breathe. Light explodes behind your eyes. They open everything. Reading every single word. You hold a perfect poker face, breath locked, ashamed at the mere glimmer of even dreaming of reading one of your poems out loud one day.

Suddenly, you're back on that plane. Pretending to sleep. Your hand hidden under your scarf, furiously scribbling a poem to alchemize whatever just happened—whatever happens every time you open your notebook. You feel power in every word, a thread pulling you back into yourself. Authentic creation, your last rebellion.

But the airport steward catches you, the special-forces agent in another mask, and leans in, drilling you for hours, asking if they'd been rough. You smiled: "Not at all."

You meant not yet.

Exhale.

Death never scared you. Being silenced did. Being blinded with rage. Because both humanitarians and poets on the frontlines must create in times of disaster.

Mohammed is still writing. And you? The peace around you shatters harder than a bomb. You feel trapped, exploding inside your own body. You were trapped in Gaza too, forced to stay, then forced to leave. If you were being authentic, you would be making an impact right now. You want to scream, but there is no sound for what detonates through every pore.

You throw the phone at the wall, but it bounces back, so you smash it again.

You feel it in your skin, disgust, the kind that settles into muscle memory. Disgust at pretending, at being a cog in the machine you swore you'd escape. Disgust at yourself for becoming a slave to the very system you wanted to reinvent, to free others from it.

Creative freedom.

Emily, you have yet again failed to deliver... What's wrong with you? You are embarrassing yourself. You have failed.

You flare up. Your skin turns electric.

Authenticity has its own timing. Its own fire. It rises through the layers of voices until you can't distinguish whether it's the donors, the bosses, or the interrogators in Lisbon, Gaza, or Tel Aviv.

Another message pings. He sent you a poem!:

O lady of the morning, grant me leave,

To let my fingers, like soft butterflies, weave

Across the meadow of your laughing ray.

Wait. It's about you… the power of poetry, and being seen, and the undeniable current between you both, beautiful, frightening, and disarming.

You type back: *Wow… You made me cry. Thank you.*

You laugh because a Muslim man in a conflict zone is the only person you could ever admit that to. How else could you say he saved your life? That he shattered your self-hatred by sending you poetry of you, art that you couldn't reject without rejecting him, the most authentic person you know. That he softened your death drive in peace, while fighting to survive in chaos himself.

He replies: *I wish you could understand Arabic to feel it as it is.* You can. You feel every syllable. His poem grounds you more than breathwork ever has.

You're not stuck because of a report. You're stuck because your truth is unsafe, punishing.

The memory flickers: the cold metallic wand tracing circles around your areolae.

"Again," she said.

Inhale.

Fire breath.

Faster.

You exhale hard until the breath takes over and you slip into its rhythm. You push too far; you always do. The copper taste of blood slides down your throat, and now pours from your nose, and still, you don't stop. You can't. But your body gives in after what feels like hours, days, and at last, finally, you surrender. You let it all in.

The poets' laughter. Their spoken word. Their electric playfulness. Their genuine love for you. Their loss, and yours. You're fearless. You've always fought. Justice always prevails. But this, fighting for your own light, is the battle you can't win. You pull threads of breathlessness, bliss, and the light that joy brings. And you remember your vision, to inspire, to give hope, and how it happens effortlessly when you are all enjoying the process. The authentic fearless you inspires poets the most, with laughter, with all of you.

He texts again: *Forty years of memories are heavy when bidding farewell to a city… How do you carry an entire city on your shoulders, then set it down to say goodbye?*

Maybe that's why the report is excruciating. You too are carrying too many stories, too many souls, too many fights all at once. The truth hits with a migraine behind your left eye.

It wasn't failure you feared. It was freedom. Freedom to feel all spectrums of light, to feel joy. You fear being seen, being read, being the poet, and all the nakedness that it asks of you. That the special forces laughed at. That everyone rejected, mocked, and gaslit your entire life. But you were never afraid to speak truth. Wake up.

Somewhere, Raghad is still writing. You picture her by candlelight, crafting lines in her little notebook about olive trees and freedom, holding onto the belief that poetry can endure beyond war. She messaged last week: *Small details, the scent of an orange, the shadow of an olive tree, carry truths that words alone cannot contain.*

And you, still struggling to lift a pen, you whisper her name into the silence, remembering that authentic creation begins simply by showing up raw and real even when it hurts. But the room closes in darker and deeper. Failure thickens. The world narrows to the sound of your pulse. This is the crux. The moment the heart breaks open.

The density.

The body.

The rawness.

You tell the poets to write into the fire.

Adrenaline spikes again, knowing that this time you need to lean in. You can't give up. Not now. Not when someone still needs you. You made a pact with yourself at her age: you will not be a wasted resource. You will not disappear, not until you make a difference. An impossible feat? Even the humanitarian world called you an idealist. At least I was being me.

You think of Raghad, young, confident, proud of her poetry, gushing to share, to be heard, to express. The other refugee girls beside her, giggling as they practiced haiku with you and Mohamed. Now their school was gone. Their world was gone. But she kept writing, holding on to the dream that if they had to die, they'd go together, not individually. And you wonder, how could you let yourself become one more disappearance in her life?

She lights up your phone: *Creativity remains the light that guides us out of darkness. I will keep writing no matter what.*

You try to breathe faster; that's what helps. You aren't just stuck; you're paralyzed. Your mind is sprinting at a million miles an hour, and your body refuses to catch up. But this only proves how trapped you are in your own body. How long has it been? A minute? A day? Darkness presses in.

Then the screen flickers alive, and Mohamed asks how you are.

You start typing: *Still breathing.* [Delete.]

Your head throbs, pain blitzing through you, but this moment matters more.

You write instead: *I'm great, so glad to hear from you! Write me a poem.* [Send.]

Your wise authentic self comes forth. Lead by example.

His words hum, vibrating through fractures, and soon your pulse falls into a rhythm. Something inside you wakes. Your spine straightens. Your breath steadies. You sit up.

You pick the phone up again, ignoring the fresh sting of glass digging into your thumb. The message pulls you in because it feels real.

Everything is shaking. Everything is on fire. His messages come rapid-fire, so you can't turn your phone off; any one of them could be his last. Your weight and weightlessness collapse into each other. You're grounded and floating at once, pulled inward to your truth and outward to him, to his world, to the collective you're both tethered to. In that raw authenticity, you exist fully, not fighting to leave, connected without losing your center.

You ask again, more softly this time, *How are you really?*

A pause. Then:

Oh, just head pains from the situation.

Your migraine becomes irrelevant. Your heart unravels, ruptures.

How can I help? Can I send you money?

Oh no, please. Money cannot help. There is no food to buy.

Something fierce rises in your chest.

Please write, you tell him. You send another prompt without thinking. Every time you ask him to write, his energy flares alive.

It's too late for us now, he says. *We really are dying.*

A chill slices through you.

Oh... or maybe you're becoming enlightened. You are accessing higher consciousness, you reply, terrified that you're minimizing a famine.

Yes! I have been meditating. Please show me how. Yes. This is why you are my soul sister.

Yes, we were meant to meet! You send him a prompt.

How are you, my sister? How are your headaches? I have been praying for you.

You rise higher instantly; you could never be the shadow version of you with a poet. He calls you back to your innate wisdom to not dwell in lower realms.

He shares more avidly: *I am lost in the novel actually... preparing folders for each character. I write poetry when overwhelmed.* Even then, there is discipline. You imagine him by the sea, sorting his thoughts into folders like sacred relics. Even his exhaustion is generative. He turns chaos into art.

You are a poet. Write a fucking poem. Your authentic self knows the only way out is in.

You open a new document titled The Authentic Poet. You stare at the blank page. How can you write about authenticity when you are not, and when it feels so one-sided? The poets are the ones living in fire, and they keep sending you poetry. You promise him you'll send something back, someday, when you can bear being fully seen.

Poets call you back to yourself. They don't require explanations. Their existence alone calls you upward. Even in darkness, they

ignite light. Even in light, they ignite depth. They can't help it. It's
who they are.

You read his poem again:

Live all you wish, and chase your fears away.

Forget not joy, nor songs along your way.

This garden rose from echoes of your cheer.

You want to thank him, but the words fail. All you can manage are
crying emojis, fragments of apology. But he stops you immediately.

*No, no cry! Just feel and smile. Apologize for what? You deserve the
best. Just read and feel it. I wish I could help you.*

Maybe authenticity isn't perfection. Maybe it's the refusal to stop
creating even after you've lost faith. You can't ignore the poems
flooding you anymore. He never saw you as someone who could
save him. Or someone he could save. He only ever saw you as a
poet.

You remember what Raghad once told you: Poetry is the life that
never fades inside me. For the first time, you believe her fully. The
first refugee poet you met changed you. The second cracked you
open and destroyed you. But this one, this time, saves you.

He simply reminded you who you were. Authenticity isn't serenity.
Or control. It's combustion.

This is the wisdom you've been circling all along: authenticity is not
merely expression, but the courage to be visible and lean into the
fire you would rather escape.

It's choosing not to dilute truth. And burning the performance of perfection that will only ever implode or explode. You are so provocative, they say.

The voice rises inside you sharp, merciless: You are pathetic. No. Not anymore. Finish the report. Publish the poems. Stop calling fear "perfection." Who cares what they think? And everyone who made fun of your "little pet poetry project."

Even if showing up proves that you're impulsive, selfish, none of it matters. Because the truth is you do care. You care too much. And that is the real problem: not allowing yourself to have fun, to write, to be seen.

So you do the only thing left. You write the truth that scares you most. You send it. The real story of missing migrant children. And for the first time in decades, something settles.

Not applause.

Not approval.

Just the quiet click of alignment.

The children spoke of joy. And before you realize, your notebook is open, and you're already pages deep into a cosmic ode. Verse after verse flows through you and feels like an exhale as the sparks fire you up at the same time. It is pure unadulterated overflow, the true wisdom of being authentic. Allowing yourself to write, to express, and to be joyfully yourself.

It opens you from within, awakens the poet you kept buried. And when the current becomes too strong to contain, you do the unthinkable: you send him one of your own.

Akasha Poetica. The poems surge like a tide. Your palms are hot. Your chest expands as if something is exploding and freeing you at the same time. It's safe to be the poet.

Hours later, his message arrives: *I went to the beach just to read your poem. No poem in the world could contain the feeling of a man moved to tears by poetry. I cried for your word, Emily.*

Authenticity isn't about being fearless. It's about feeling it all and using it all as fuel. Fear is excitement without breath.

Another message floods in: *I see you as a celestial being radiant, dancing through the cosmos, crowned with daisies and narcissus. Your hair moves like planets; your eyes conduct the universe.*

Your entire body is tingling with electric currents igniting every single molecule. But in a good way. He writes of stars while his city burns.

One more lands as revelation: *Do you know why the human soul longs for eternity? Because only there can it find someone who understands it completely.*

This is remembrance, not romance, recognition. The kind that dissolves all that is not in alignment, bodily and bodiless, and leaves only light, pure, unfiltered, undeniable. And suddenly the same question from those old interrogation rooms echoes back through you: Who are you really working for?

His last line arrives without hesitation: *Remain here always, that I may write the stars.*

How did he know? How did he speak straight into the truth you've never said aloud? The candle beside you flickers alive again. Outside, the wind roars like it knows your name.

Because the poets don't write for validation, nor escape, they write from truth, from the marrow of experience, from the light that refuses extinction. And so do you.

Fully.

Unapologetically.

Authentically yourself.

You are a poet.

"Today you are You, that is truer than true. There is no one alive who is You-er than You."

— Dr. Seuss

She Loved First: A Story of Authenticity, Devotion and Coming Home to the Self

∞∞C∞∞

By Fiona Marie Williams

A Love Letter to the Girl Who Gave Her Heart Before She Knew What It Might Cost

To the girl who loved first—
before she understood how to,
before she knew it could break her,
before she believed she had to prove she was worthy of it.

You never truly lost her.
You only forgot how real she was.
This is your invitation back—
to truth,
to love,
to the most unfiltered, honest version of you.

The Moment I Remembered Who I was

A remembering of who I was—before the performance, before the proving, before I ever believed I had to earn love.

We talk a lot about authenticity these days.
About "being yourself."
Living in alignment.
Owning your voice.
Standing in your truth.
But what if authenticity isn't something we *become*?
What if it's something we *remember*?

What if it's not about adding more—
but about gently undoing what was never ours to carry?

What if the truest thing about you…
is the way you loved before you knew the cost?
Before the world told you to become anything else?

That's what happened to me.

One quiet afternoon, after a phone call with my brother—
someone I hadn't felt truly connected to in years—
something opened in my chest.
Not a thought.
Not a memory.
A frequency.

A remembering.

I remembered who I was before I tried to become someone.
Before I fixed others just to feel safe.
Before I bent myself for approval
or chased connection in places that couldn't hold it.

I remembered the first time I *loved.*

Not the first time I was loved—
but the first time I *gave* love.
Freely.
Innocently.
Without needing anything in return.

It was the day my brother was born.

And from that moment on, without even knowing it,
I spent decades trying to recreate that feeling—
offering my heart to people who felt like the moment
that love stopped being received.

I believed if I just gave more,
stayed soft,
held it all together…
maybe love would return.

It didn't.

Until I stopped.
Until I said *no more.*
Until I remembered:
Love doesn't need to be earned.
And authenticity doesn't require suffering.

Authenticity is what's left
when we stop betraying ourselves.

This book isn't a manual.
It's a remembering.
A return to the wisdom beneath our masks—
the wisdom of who we've always been.

It's also a love letter.
To the little girl who gave love
before she knew what it cost.
And to the woman who finally remembered:

I never needed to be *more.*
I only needed to come home.

The Day I Remembered I Loved First

How a single moment of presence cracked open a truth I didn't
know I'd been carrying all my life.

I didn't expect it to return this way.
Not through a flood of memories or an old photograph.
But during an ordinary phone call—a quiet reconnection with my
brother after years of silence.

I was just listening.
He was just talking.
Nothing dramatic. Nothing profound.

I simply offered something real—an unfiltered piece of my heart.

And for the first time in years, he received it with grace.

After we hung up, something deep inside me softened.
I remembered.
I had loved him first.

Not out of duty.
Not because someone told me to.

But because the moment he was born, something ancient and true stirred awake inside me—a feeling I couldn't name back then. But I know now what it was.

It was love in its purest form.
Unfiltered.
Unproven.
Unattached.
Just a little girl, seeing her baby brother for the first time, instinctively offering her heart.

Not to gain anything.
Not to become anything.
Just because love wanted to move through her.

And in that quiet moment, years later, as I set the phone down, I realized something I'd long forgotten:

My first experience of love wasn't in being loved.
It was in giving it.

Freely.
Fully.
Without fear.
Without performance.
With pure presence.

And from that day on, I began the long journey back to that version of myself.
Not realizing how often I would confuse love with effort.
How many times I would give my heart to those who couldn't hold it.

How I would seek out distorted reflections of that first imprint—
all in the name of reclaiming an innocence I once knew.

This book is about that return.
About the moment I remembered who I was when I loved first.
About the woman I became through that remembering.
And the vow I made when I finally came home to her:

Never again will I give love where it cannot be received.
Never again will I forget that my love is sacred.

If you've ever over-given…
If you've ever mistaken effort for intimacy…
If you've ever chased the feeling of home in the arms of someone
who could never offer it—

This book is for you.

Because maybe, like me, you forgot you loved first.
And maybe, like me, you're finally ready to remember.

Love is our collective, authentic truth—
And when we remember that truth,
we return to the wisdom of authenticity—
the knowing that real love asks for nothing but presence.

The First Love – My Brother's Birth
The innocence of a child's heart—the moment love moved through
me freely for the very first time.

I don't remember the day in a linear way.
There's no timestamp. No clear scene I can replay like a movie.
But there's a frequency I'll never forget.

Something shifted in the air the moment he arrived.
And something inside me shifted too.

I knew little about the world at that point.
But I knew what I felt in my body—
a soft, instinctive pull toward him.
A pure desire to love.

Not because anyone told me to.
Not because it was expected.
But because it felt like the most natural thing in the world.

Here he was—tiny, pure, untouched.
And something in me just opened.
Like love had been asleep in my chest, and his presence woke it up.

I remember wanting to give him everything:
My attention. My toys. My protection. My joy.
Not to play the part of the "good big sister"—
but because I wanted him to feel safe, seen, and loved.

And giving him that love?

It felt good.
It felt whole.
It felt real.
It felt like home.

And in that homecoming, I brushed up against something ancient—
the quiet wisdom of authenticity.
The kind that lives in our earliest, unfiltered expressions of love.

Of course, we fought.
We pushed and pulled like siblings do.
But we always came back.
That was the magic of our bond—it didn't hold grudges.
It remembered love more than it remembered conflict.

So I kept offering it.
Soft love. Fierce love. Forgiving love.
It became a blueprint I didn't know I was building.

Give love. Come back. Keep giving.

What I didn't realize until much later was this:
That experience was my first energetic imprint of love.

It left a frequency in my body—
that love is safe.
That love is home.
That love just is.

But life changed.
My brother stopped receiving my love in the same way.
And later, betrayal cracked the safety I once knew—
not from him, but from the first boy I gave my heart to.

When I was met with disconnection, avoidance, shutdown,
rejection—
something in me panicked.

I believed if I just gave more,
they'd love me back.
Just like I loved them.

All I had was the memory of that first love.
So I tried to recreate it—again and again.
In places where it was never safe.
With people who weren't capable.

All in an effort to feel that feeling again.

Because the truth is:
I didn't just love my brother.
I loved how it felt to love him.

But the wisdom of authenticity?
It can't be forced.
It only rises when we stop trying to earn what was once given
freely.

And that became the foundation I built my entire understanding of
love on.

Where love became effort.
Where I learned to chase what was never meant to hold me.

There wasn't one defining moment.
It didn't shatter all at once.

But over time, something between us changed.
He got older.
I did too.
Life layered its noise.
And the quiet, sacred thread between us stretched.

We still loved each other—
but something had shifted.

He stopped letting me in the same way.
Stopped needing me.
Stopped responding to love like it was something to return.

The space between us no longer felt true.
And the wisdom of authenticity began to fade.

And I didn't know what to do with that.

Because my entire understanding of love was built on this:

If I love you,
and I keep loving you,
you'll soften.
You'll open.
You'll receive it—
just like he used to.

Because that's what love felt like at the beginning:
Being myself was enough.
Authentic. Unfiltered.
Me—without fear.

But over time, I started believing love had to be proven.

If it wasn't landing, I must not be doing enough.
If I just loved better, softer, harder—maybe I'd be received again.

So I carried that imprint with me.

Into male friendships.
Into romantic partners.
Into people who could not meet me.

But they felt familiar—
because they mirrored the moment love first turned into effort.

I didn't choose them because they were healthy.
I chose them because my body recognized the ache.

That ache became my compass.
And my devotion became my drug.

But the deeper truth was this:

I had confused effort with intimacy.
And that confusion came at the cost of my authenticity.

Because the wisdom of authenticity isn't about how much you
give—
it's about whether you're giving from truth or from fear.

There is power in knowing when love is no longer true to you.

Still, I kept choosing people I could help.
People I could love so deeply
that maybe—just maybe—they'd feel it enough to change.
To open.
To return.
But they didn't.
Because they couldn't.

And the more I gave to places where it wasn't safe,
the more I lost pieces of myself.

Until one day, I woke up exhausted.
From giving.
From proving.

From trying to recreate purity
in places where distortion ruled.

I couldn't see it clearly at the time.
But what I was really doing was this:

I was trying to recreate the first time I loved.
The first time it felt clean.
The first time it felt safe.

By offering that same love
to people who reminded me of the moment it broke.

**Love returns
when you offer it to yourself first.**

When you listen to the quiet ache of your heart
and let your authentic truth burn so brightly
it no longer seeks permission to exist.

When your love becomes enough—
not because they receive it,
but because you finally do.

The partner who reflected everything I hadn't yet healed—
he became the catalyst for my return.

By the time I met him,
I had already mastered the art
of loving people who couldn't fully receive it.

I didn't know I was doing it.

It felt romantic.
It felt familiar.
It felt like devotion.
It even felt authentic—
because I had confused authenticity with self-sacrifice.

But it wasn't love.
Not the kind I gave my brother.
Not the kind that was free.

It was effort.
It was attachment dressed as loyalty.
It was trying to earn safety
from someone whose nervous system couldn't offer it.

He met me spiritually—
but often bypassed the places where real intimacy lives.

He could speak the language of the soul,
but struggled to sit with the rawness of human emotion.
Compassion. Understanding.

He was brilliant—
wise, visionary, magnetic, spiritual, influential.

But beneath all that light
was the same pattern I had known for years:

A closed heart.
Avoidant energy.
Unreliable presence.
Insight offered in place of intimacy.
Projection.

Silence where there should have been repair.
Withdrawal when I needed warmth.

And my body recognized it.
Not as danger...
but as home.

So I did what I always did:
I tried to love him better.
I gave. I opened. I held.
I stretched my softness to meet his walls.

I used every healing tool I had ever learned.
Every breath.
Every insight.
Every practice I had mastered.

I believed that if I could stay soft enough,
fierce enough,
strong enough,
forgiving enough,
loving enough,
understanding enough...
then maybe—just maybe—
love would return to me like it did in the beginning.

But love isn't something you earn.
And authenticity isn't about bending to be chosen—
it's about standing rooted in who you are
and remembering:
Real love never asks you to abandon yourself.

No matter what I did,
I was never fully met.
Not clearly.
Not steadily.
Not with the depth I longed for.

And it broke me.
Again and again.

Until I saw the truth:

He wasn't harming me.
He was reflecting back the part of me
that still believed I had to do something to be loved.
He became the mirror I didn't want to look into—
the one that revealed my distortion,
my self-abandonment,
my compulsion to give love where it wasn't safe.

He wasn't the problem.
He was the pattern.

And seeing that—naming it, honoring it, releasing it—
was one of the wisest things I've ever done.
Because the wisdom of authenticity
is the ability to see clearly, even when it hurts.

One day, my body finally said:
Enough.

Not from anger.
Not from collapse.
But from clarity.

From truth.

I remembered what real love felt like.
Our puppy, Buddy, reminded me.
When he arrived, my heart cracked open
in a way I hadn't felt in years.

No performance.
No effort.
Just presence.
Just unconditional love.

He showed me what true love feels like:
No proving. No fixing. No sacrificing.
Just presence. Just being. Just love.

And I knew:
This wasn't it.
This wasn't love—
at least not the kind I wanted to live in.

So I let go.
Not just of him—
but of the belief that love must be earned.
That it means fixing, bending, shrinking, self-abandoning.

I ended the relationship with a clean, unapologetic "No."
Complete.

And something inside me cracked open.

Not grief.
Not regret.

But space.

Space for something deeper.
Something quieter.
Something truer.
Something that had always been mine—
before the bending,
before the proving.

Something whole.
Something wise.
Something wildly and unmistakably… authentic.

It was the wisdom of authenticity returning home to my body.

Free.

When love finally returned—clean, real, and unearned—
I wasn't expecting it.
I had no narrative in my mind.
No plan to receive what came next.

After that final "no,"
the energetic cut,
the full reclamation—
I was raw.
But I was clear.
Open in a way I hadn't been in years.

I wasn't waiting for someone to rush in.
I was letting my nervous system exhale.
Letting the old ache dissolve.

And then…

My brother called.

We hadn't spoken like that in years.
Not soulfully.
Not freely.
Not without tension.

But this time was different.

He spoke.
I listened.
He shared his world.
And I didn't offer advice—I offered presence.

For the first time in my life,
I saw him not as someone I needed to fix,
but as a man on his own path.
Capable. Whole. Ready.

I offered something from my heart.
And this time, he received it.
He moved with it.
Just like that.

Something in me let go.
Collapsed into grace.
Into something real.
A remembering—
felt, not forced.

He received me.
Without resistance.
Without projection.
Without bypass.

It was simple.
It was sacred.

Then came the memory.
Not a thought—a frequency.

I remembered the first time I loved him.
When he was born.
When I gave love freely,
without fear,
without needing anything in return.
Because it was natural.
Because it was real.

That's what I had forgotten:
When authenticity fades,
love becomes performance.
Joy becomes fleeting.
Peace becomes something we strive to earn.

But for the first time since childhood,
he met me in that place again.

So, I wrote him a poem.
I sent it without expecting anything back.

He replied:
"That's really nice. It made me tear up a bit haha."

That was it.
And it was everything.

Not dramatic.
Not spiritualized.
Just real.

I didn't need to explain it.
The transmission had already landed.

Love had returned.
Not from a partner.
Not from fantasy.
But from the first person I ever loved.

And this time,
he was open to it—
because I had stopped trying to change him.
Because I had stopped trying to prove anything.
Because I simply loved.
Without condition.
Without effort.
Just presence.

The sacred promise I made—to never abandon myself again,
and to only give love where it can truly land.

I will never again give love where it cannot be received.

Not because I've hardened,
not because I've lost my softness,
but because I finally remember who I am
when I'm not trying to prove it.

I don't need to be needed.
I don't need to be chosen.
I don't need to prop up what someone else keeps dropping.

My love is not a performance.
It is a frequency.
And it is sacred—because it is authentic.

I now understand that the ache I felt in so many relationships
wasn't because they were bad people—
but because I was trying to relive a purity
in places that were never safe enough for it to survive.

I forgive myself for staying too long.
For giving too much.
For thinking my light could melt someone's armor.

I vow to never again abandon myself in the name of connection.

I vow to give from fullness.
To love from truth.
To rest when it's not met.
To walk away with grace when I feel distortion.
To protect my softness with sacred boundaries.

I vow to carry the wisdom of authenticity into every choice I
make—
even when it's uncomfortable,
even when it means choosing to walk away.

I vow to honor the little girl who loved her little brother with a
wide-open heart—
not because she had to,

but because that's who she was.
The most authentic part of me, all along.

And I vow to live as her now.
Not chasing,
not proving,
but simply being what she always was:

Love that remembers itself.

What we forget. What we perform. What we remember.
What we become when we stop betraying ourselves.
What I now know.

And this, perhaps, is the greatest wisdom of authenticity…

Authenticity isn't loud.
It doesn't need to be proven.
It isn't about how much of yourself you share—
but how true you are when no one's watching.

Authenticity is the frequency of the original self—before
performance, before protection, before pain.

And most of us lose it early.
Not by choice—but by survival.

We lose it the first time love is withheld.
When softness is shamed.
When being "too much" or "too emotional" gets us pushed away.
We start shape-shifting.
Becoming palatable.
Becoming useful.

Becoming what others can handle.

And so, without realizing it,
we build entire lives on top of a self that isn't fully us.

I became the giver.
The understanding one.
The woman who would stay through shutdown, projection, and
spiritual bypass—
as long as there was a hope that love would be returned.

But that's not authenticity.
That's survival love disguised as devotion.

Authenticity is what remains when the distortion falls away.
It's the voice you hear when you stop over-explaining.
It's the knowing in your body when something just isn't clean.
It's the courage to choose peace over potential.

Authenticity is the moment you remember:

"I was love before they told me who I needed to be."
"I was worthy before they failed to meet me."
"And I can stop trying to earn what I already am."

To reclaim your authenticity is to stop abandoning yourself in the
name of connection.
To no longer seek softness in places that feel hard.
To no longer try to be understood by people who have no intention
of truly seeing you.
To return to the original frequency you were born with:

Truth.
Love.
Wholeness.
Without performance.

A moment to pause and ask yourself: When did I first love without fear—and how can I return to that frequency now? Return to your own remembering.

Now, it's your turn.
Not to copy my story—
but to remember your own.
The one that's been quietly waiting for you to listen.
The one that holds the wisdom of your authenticity.

Find a quiet space.
Place your hands on your heart.
Close your eyes.
And ask:

"When was the first time I loved before I knew how?"

Maybe it was a sibling.
A parent.
A pet.
A tree.
Yourself.

Let it come.

Let the frequency—not the memory—rise.

And from that place, complete this sentence:

"I was love when..."

Write it.
Feel it.
Return to it.

Then, if it feels true, speak this aloud:

I vow to remember who I was before I believed I had to be anything else.

I vow to no longer give love where it cannot land.
I vow to honor the version of me who loved first,
and to become the version who never forgets that she is love.
I vow to lead, live, and love from my original truth—
not because I need to be chosen, but because I've already chosen me.

May the girl who loved first—and the boy who didn't know how to hold it—both remember how to meet in open-hearted, authentic, and freely given love.

And now, as you close these pages—
may you feel the pulse of your original love.
May you stop offering it to places that can't hold it.
May you no longer prove what you are.
May you remember the frequency you came in with.
May your love be sacred, soft, and sovereign—
a reflection of your most authentic self.

You don't have to become anything.
Just return.

You are already.
You are the one who loved first.

Or him.
The part of you that never stopped loving—
only forgot how safe it was to stay…
to let love in, and allow it to be returned.

And now, you both remember.

"**Authenticity is the courage to be yourself in a world that constantly tells you to be someone else.**"

— Unknown

Truth Can Hurt

⊸∘◠◡◠∘⊸

By Jason Bart

"**W**hat the fuck…"

That's all I had time to say before instinct took over and I clamped down on the brakes of my green and black Honda VTR250. It was late and rainy, the road covered in the kind of wet that makes it look slicker than it should. The first rain of the season had pulled up oil, rising from the bitumen, the whole street shining like a sunset over a calm ocean beneath the orange glow of streetlights. One wrong move and the ground would be waiting.

And the wrong move came. I know not to reactively squeeze the brakes… yet I did react.

It only took the slightest force on the front brake for my front wheel to lock in an instant. My trusted bike went from upright and alive to sideways and sliding on the surface quicker than I could say "… are you doing, bro?"

The sound of metal scraping against bitumen cut through the rain, then the violent thud of my chest slamming into the front corner of the white Toyota that had just pulled out.

I spun. My body ricocheted, twisted, and slid across the road until it all came to a stop. I lay there, helmet on, rain coming down, the world blurry through the visor. Over and over, I muttered in shock, "What the fuck?! What the fuck?!"

Time went weird. Seconds or minutes passed, I don't know. When I finally lifted my head, I saw the car I'd collided with, headlights sparkling across the wet road. I locked eyes with the driver through the glass, even though I knew he couldn't hear me, I finished the statement again from my gut, "What the fuck are you doing, bro?!"

I wasn't alone for long. Out of the dark, a group of men appeared; three, maybe four. They pulled their cars over, jumped out, and ran toward me in the rain. No hesitation. No care for the traffic they were jamming up for others. Just brothers moving instinctively to help.

As the men around me helped however they could, I noticed something else. Brotherhood. Presence. The way strangers will drop everything to make sure another man doesn't bleed out alone in the dark.

That, too, was authenticity. These men weren't following a script or waiting for permission. They acted. They showed up. No roles, no titles, just men in the rain doing what was needed.

In that raw moment, I saw a mirror of what's possible in me, too: the capacity to respond authentically when life calls me to shift gears. To be present, grounded, and dependable in the new rhythm. To be the man who stops, assesses the situation, and dances to the music of the moment.

One of them crouched beside me, checking if I was conscious, if I could breathe. Two others lifted my bike off the road and dragged the twisted mess to the side. Someone else guided the driver to the side of the road and calmly took charge, starting a WhatsApp group to swap details. It was surreal, lying there in pain and seeing men I didn't know show up like that for me, present, reliable, and solid.

Something was happening, I could feel it in my bones, beyond the obvious, there was an invitation to look deeper into my surroundings.

I love you, brothers, I thought, as they supported me to the side of the road, with my chest short of breath, and the right side of my body throbbing. *There are good men in the world. I see you. I appreciate you.*

This wasn't my first bike accident. You don't ride for years without a few spills. But this was the first time I'd collided with another vehicle, and let me tell you, it hurts!

The irony is, I'd been cautious all night. I am not a fan of riding in the rain, and I didn't have wet-weather gear with me. Just my leather jacket, jeans, and work shoes: poor armor against a car crash. I'd been keeping my distance, slowing down near intersections, doing all the "right" things. I was less than ten minutes from home when I saw the traffic backing up on both sides near the railway crossing. I slowed as my gut told me something could go wrong.

And then, of course, it did.

The Toyota up ahead needed to cross the road in front of me, so it inched forward, then stopped. *Good*, I thought, *They've seen me.* When I was only ten meters out, he pulled across in front of me and my world flipped on its head. Literally.

"What the fuck…"

When it comes to authenticity, it isn't about sugar-coating life or putting a neat spin on the shit that hurts so that I look like I am at ease. It's about feeling the discomfort and looking to see where and why it is presenting itself. My truth can come out in ways that are pretty messy, painful, and raw. My truth at that moment was simple: there is something I don't want to see. What is it?

Often, on a journey to Truth, I start at a place of absolute doubt. It feels like the world's lost its bearings, and I don't know which way to turn. And this was one of those moments. I mean, talk about a pattern interrupt!

Within 30 minutes of the accident, I arrived home safely with my girlfriend who had just finished teaching a birthing yoga class and was already on her way to her car as soon as she saw my simple text message, "Can you call me when you can?" Knowing something was up, she came straight to get me and then took me home to clean up and rest before going to see the doctor in the morning.

Feeling confident that nothing appeared to be broken and the chest pain was subsiding from the impact with the car, I was also confident there was no internal bleeding. I am not one for waiting in hospitals, and going to the doctor the next day ended up sufficient to diagnose the shoulder and knee damage, along with back and other abrasions.

I have a belief, one that has been shown to me more than once. It's that what I experience in the outer world is a mirror of what's moving inside me. That the sights, sounds, synchronicities, and even accidents aren't random. They reflect the state of my being, pointing me either toward my natural resonance of ease and grace, with a spice of joy, or away from it. And right now, with my body bruised and my ego battered, I am a long way from ease, grace, and joy!

Somatics and many traditions speak about polarity in the body, where the right side is often linked with the masculine, strength, action, and stability, and the left with the feminine, receptivity, nurturing, and intuition.

And here I was: My right shoulder over-extended, right knee injured, some heavy scars. My masculine side was severely compromised. My feminine, on the other hand, was slightly grazed and fine.

The body language was clear: your masculine is taking a hit.

The timing wasn't subtle. Just hours before the accident, I'd said yes to stepping into a new role at my recent full-time job, Studio Director for a brand I have loved since I was seven years old.

Fast-forward decades, I was being offered the chance to lead a retail outlet representing this brand, just as it celebrates its 100th year in existence. For the boy in me, it was a dream checked off the bucket list. For the man in me, it promised stability, recognition, and financial security; things that mattered even more now that I was becoming a grandfather.

So, I said yes. Out loud. To the owner, to myself, to the opportunity. I was saying yes to the steady paycheck and being the steward of a brand I'd loved more than any other.

There was an obvious discord within me—the rebel, the entrepreneur, and maybe a bit of the adolescent in me, was very unhappy! Feeling chained to responsibility and locked back into the system.

This is where the wisdom of authenticity begins. Not in comfort, but in the collision. Not in the pretty pictures of the IG life and polished words, but in the realizations that are right there in front of me. Not in pretending everything's fine, but in admitting, out loud, if I need to, "What the fuck is happening?"

From embracing the belief that the world is reflecting back to me, I realized that the world speaks to all of us. First with a gentle whisper. Then it raises its voice. If we still don't listen, it can become more literal, more corporal, and even knock us flat, sometimes on the road, and in my case, right into the path of a car. Talk about deaf!

The truth of the accident wasn't just that a driver didn't see me, or, as he told me, "I didn't even look." It was that something in me was unseen, too. Something in my masculine, my freedom, my direction was about to be slammed into, and the world delivered it with headlights and steel.

Because inquiry is the doorway to truth. And if I walk through it honestly, it leads me straight into the wisdom of my authenticity.

Part of me genuinely wanted that yes. I wanted the honor of representing the brand. I wanted the routine in life, the stability it created, the safety. However, another part of me felt the trap closing in the moment the words left my lips.

A cage. A loss of sovereignty. A loss of freedom.

Not because the role itself was wrong; it was because something in me knew the cost. The freedom I prized, the spontaneity, the ability to chart my own course, to follow my soul's work, felt like it was being put on a leash.

And my masculine, the part of me that thrives on adventure, freedom, and self-direction, was the one taking the hit. First in my psyche, then in my body.

This is where the wisdom of authenticity cuts deeper. It isn't just about asking "What do I want?" It's about asking, "Which part of me is speaking? Which part of me is saying yes and which part is screaming no?"

Because those parts coexist. Ignoring the scream doesn't make it go away. It just makes it louder and more conniving.

After the accident, once the shock wore off, I started to hear the inner scream more clearly. It wasn't just a no. It was a roar.

The rebel in me, the anarchist, the bratty kid in the backseat yelling, "Fuck you, I won't do what you tell me!" That voice was alive and thrashing. Beneath it, the scared little boy, hoping he was cool enough, strong enough, worthy enough to be loved.

Freedom for that backseat kid meant no responsibility. I can do whatever I want. No rules. No ties. No commitments. Just pure sovereignty, unrestrained. Anarchy.

And fair enough. That part deserves to be seen and acknowledged. And, I also knew, I can't hand the Peter Pan in me the steering wheel of my life. He's definitely not fit to drive. He will drive it off a cliff and fly away from the wreckage and completely forget that it was there.

Authenticity isn't just about being in the moment and oblivious to the world around. It doesn't mean giving every voice inside me equal power.

It does mean having the awareness to recognise the various parts of myself, to be able to truly validate them, and take what is being said into consideration in the totality of the moment.

And in this case, as I didn't listen to the whispers, it built up to a scream, and it was violent enough to throw me off a bike.

There I was, saying yes to an opportunity aligned with one part of me, and another was dressing up as self-destruction for realization. Knocking me down to stop me from walking into what they considered a trap.

What if I lose my freedom? What if I get trapped? What if I can't get out?

Fear spins those futures until they look like facts. And suddenly, I'm lying on the road with a busted shoulder and knee, convinced I'm about to sacrifice my soul.

The wisdom of authenticity is outside the story. It is the natural state. It has nothing to prove. A deeper question: is this fear actually true, or is it my ego throwing a tantrum? The scream in me was terrified of losing freedom. So, I need to define what freedom really is.

For years, my fantasy definition of freedom was the cliché one: travel the world, teach workshops, live online, hit festivals, do whatever I want, whenever I want. And I did taste that lifestyle once. For a moment, it felt like everything.

But freedom shouldn't be a fantasy, available to just a few. Freedom should be a natural state of being.

The definition of freedom has changed quite a bit for me recently. Once upon a time, freedom was closely related to the avoidance of responsibility.

Now, freedom is not about being free from responsibility; it's about being free *in* responsibility. It's the way that I am, in my response, that makes me free. To be able to respond to life's demands with ease, grace, and action, rather than resentment, fear, and being frozen.

That's living from authenticity. To have the emotional intelligence, and maybe even the energetic intelligence, to be witness to what is happening in the mind, heart, and soul within.

To meet reality on its own terms, not run from it. To dance with the actual music playing, not the song I wish was on.

So, if the role of Studio Director gives me stability, allows me to protect and provide for my family, and lets me honor a brand that shaped me since childhood, then maybe that's not a trap. Maybe that is a way to find freedom in a new form.

I remember my darkest days, when I wanted to say no to everything. I was fighting the system, rejecting commitments. I was forcing people to believe the Matrix was evil, and maybe it is. I'd convinced myself that to stay free, I had to stay unbound. Yet all that did was leave me bound to my own fear of losing freedom.

My self-sabotage is real. I create havoc, make excuses, and blow up opportunities, all so I wouldn't have to risk failing. And underneath it all was the belief that I wasn't enough. That I wasn't worthy.

And by going through all of that, I was eventually forced to find something deeper.

I was reminded of a day that had a huge impact on my life. I was about to separate from my wife and kids, and this was one of my last days at home. I was alone in the backyard, balancing and dancing with a glass ball. It felt like a meditation for me. The sun was shining down on the glass ball and refracting light onto a point on my hand. Not enough to burn, and enough to feel the warmth. This image somehow made me question: Where is my flame?

Our chi, or life force, can be seen as an inner flame, and I wondered how mine was doing. As you can imagine, I was not in the best place emotionally, and when I tried to visualize my inner flame, I saw only a pile of ash. Like the leftovers of a big bonfire the night before. I swept away some of the ash, looking to see if there were still embers underneath. There was the defining glow still alive in the heart of the fire, deeply needing some fuel. I imagined myself laying kindling gently onto the embers, building up this fire within me, and vowed never to be so absent from my inner flame again.

It sounds a bit strange, though that is exactly what it looks like. My soul's source. The fire that burns inside of me. It's my responsibility to ensure that it doesn't get trapped or suffocated. Part of me saw this job as a giant wet blanket about to be thrown on my fire, and I was scared.

For this inner fire to be burning freely and cleanly is a sign that things are in alignment in life. That is authenticity. Being able to witness when my flame is burning clearly is where the wisdom is integrated.

As a result, I realized freedom isn't about making sure I am never in a cage. It's about knowing I carry the flame with me wherever I go, and how well I show up in ease and grace in every moment, which indicates how close I am to living in freedom. Even in what could be seen as mundane tasks and responsibilities or even in long-term relationships and commitments.

That's authenticity. To live from that flame, not from fear.

The accident was my body's way of forcing me to look at my flame. Making sure I didn't just rush into the role without examining what it cost me. It was painful as pedagogy. Bruises as teachers.

And that, to me, is the gift of authenticity. Being pulled back to myself.

It doesn't come wrapped in neat packages. It comes as rain-slick bitumen, as a smashed bike, as a knee that won't bend, and a shoulder that won't lift. It comes as fear disguised as freedom, rebellion disguised as sovereignty, ego disguised as wisdom.

The gift of truth is this: if I'm willing to listen, the world shows me exactly where I'm out of alignment, exactly where I'm resisting, and exactly where I'm called to go deeper.

The wisdom of authenticity isn't just hearing both the yes and the no. It's holding both, feeling the tension, and then stepping forward anyway, not from fear, not from fantasy, but from an inner flame.

And that's where the integration begins.

The accident left me with more than bruises. It left me with questions.

Who am I when my freedom feels threatened?
Who am I when responsibility calls?
Who am I when my body screams no but my heart whispers yes?

And most importantly: what is my authentic truth at this moment of my life?

There's a phenomenon in physics called sympathetic harmonics. Place a room full of pendulum clocks close together, each swinging at its own pace. Over time, the largest and most stable pendulum gradually pulls the others into sync. Its rhythm dominates, and the room eventually finds harmony.

Authenticity works the same way.

When I stand in my truth, grounded and resonant, I become that grandfather pendulum to myself. My frequency stabilizes and everything around me, including my family, my work, and my relationships, are invited into alignment with it.

That's the real weight of becoming a grandfather, too. Not just the title, but the responsibility of being that steady presence. The one whose vibration others can rest against. The one that is safe for the children and their children to be supported by.

"There is no place safer than on the belly of a King."

That image has stayed with me, the young child lying on the grandfather's chest, feeling the slow, steady rhythm of his grandfather's breath, knowing the world is safe because he is safe, because he is the King. That is masculinity at its most authentic: not domineering, not reckless, but stable, protective, and deeply present.

The accident showed me where my masculine had been fractured. The work afterwards was to rebuild it in resonance with this deeper truth.

Freedom is knowing I can choose responsibility without losing myself. Freedom is showing up for my family, my work, my commitments, not because I'm trapped, but because I've decided from the truth within me that this is the walk I choose to take in the world. Freedom is knowing I carry my inner flame wherever I go, and nothing can extinguish it.

When I said yes to the Studio Director role, part of me feared I was handing over my freedom. When in truth, I was actually being asked to evolve my definition of freedom. From an immature belief that sovereignty is about avoiding responsibility, to one where understanding my ability to respond gives me more freedom to embody it with grace, allowing my radiance to shine through all that I do.

That's authenticity: the courage to update our definitions when life demands us to evolve.

One of the greatest ways I can create safety as a man is through presence. To be self-aware, self-assured, and clear in my direction. Not just for me, but for everyone around me.

The accident reminded me how fragile it all is. A few seconds, a wet road, and it could've been the end. That fragility isn't meant to paralyze me; it's designed to sharpen me. To remind me that my presence matters, that every moment is an opportunity to show up as the steady pendulum, the safe belly of the king.

That's the wisdom of authenticity in action. To bring presence not just when life is comfortable, but when it's messy, painful, or terrifying. To meet the chaos with clarity and groundedness, so others can feel safe too.

If authenticity is truth expressed, then love is its companion.

For most of my life, I carried the story of not being enough. That if I didn't achieve, didn't prove, didn't live up to some fantasy version of myself, I wouldn't be worthy of love. That story fed my fear, my resistance, my rebellion.

But through somatic practice, through listening to my body, through moving with my pain rather than against it, I've come to a different place.

Enoughness isn't earned. It's fostered. Right here, right now, in this bruised and imperfect body, I am enough. And when I can stand in that truth, love flows naturally. I can begin to love myself more, and then naturally others.

Authenticity, I've come to believe, is the highest frequency of love. Because authenticity is love expressed: love for self, love for truth, love for life as it actually is. And there can be no greater wisdom than what comes through us authentically.

Life is a dance. And authenticity means learning to hear the beat of life itself and finding my steps within it.

Sometimes that means improvising. Sometimes it means discipline. Sometimes it means surrendering to a rhythm I would not have chosen.

The accident was a harsh reminder: I'd been dancing out of sync. My body hit the pavement to pull me back into rhythm. And as painful as that was, it was also a gift. Now, I can choose to move differently.

So, where does all of this leave me?

With a busted shoulder and knee, yes. With a story I'll never forget. More than that, it has left me with clarity.

The wisdom that came through me authentically, as I was looking at these wounded or immature aspects of myself, showed me that there is still resistance within me to creating stability and groundedness, which I had called being trapped.

It was that my body and the world around me are always speaking. That my fear, my rebellion, my fantasies of freedom are part of me but not the whole of me. That authenticity means listening to all those voices, then choosing from the flame at my center that continually invites me to expand.

It means becoming the steady pendulum, the safe belly of the king. It means embracing responsibility as an expression of freedom, not a theft of it. It means loving myself as enough, even in the mess, and extending that love outward through presence. And most of all, it means learning to hear the whispers, so the world doesn't have to shout.

The accident could've killed me. Accidents involving motorbikes and cars rarely end with the rider walking away. But I walked away. Battered, bruised, alive, and reflective.

That survival is itself the gift. The chance to tell the story. The chance to integrate wisdom. The chance to live differently.

Authenticity isn't a destination. It's a posture, a frequency, a practice. It's the willingness to tell the truth, even when it's messy. To listen to the body, the whispers, the accidents. To show up in resonance with who I really am, not who I'm pretending to be.

That night on the wet road was brutal. And it was sacred. It was life delivering me back to myself, back to authenticity, back to the flame, where my deeper wisdom speaks from.

And for that, even through the pain, I'm forever grateful. Because this, all of it, is the Wisdom of Authenticity.

"Your life begins again the moment you choose authenticity over acceptance."

— Unknown

AUTHOR BIOGRAPHIES

Kiki Ypsilanti

Kiki was born in Greece during an autumn morning in the 80s, being the first child of a newly formed family. She grew up a tomboy with blonde hair and deep green, curious eyes. She used to be a confidant of her girlfriends.

Always active and a life enthusiast, Kiki grew up in a small Greek town, where mountains and green forests were her best friends and visited them often with her bicycle. As an empath and a people pleaser, Kiki learned from a very young age that she had to sacrifice her true personality for safety and survival.

Helping others came to her as second nature, so she always felt like a healer. That led her down the path to medicine, studying Dentistry and becoming a certified Dental Surgeon with a specialty in Periodontology. Kiki graduated from the Greek Dental School of Aristotle University in Thessaloniki with excellence and then moved permanently to Cyprus, the home country of her future husband. There, they started their own family and she became a mother of two daughters, a well-known periodontist with a private clinic, and an integrated member of the local society, always enthusiastic and seeking the truth.

After twenty years as a gum surgeon, she transitioned into a new role as The Mind Surgeon, a certified Rapid Transformational Hypnotherapist, helping people heal from the inside out by eliminating invisible mental bacteria and transforming their lives, not just their smiles.

More recently, Kiki is discovering her true self as a writer. This is just the beginning...

website: https://www.kikiypsilanti.com/
email: contact@kikiypsilanti.com

Instagram:
the_mind_surgeon_?utm_source=qr&igshid=MThlNWY1MzQwN
A==

LinkedIn:
https://www.linkedin.com/company/the-mind-surgeon/

Facebook:
https://www.facebook.com/profile.php?id=61552488026190

David Hiscox

David Hiscox was born and raised in Western Australia. He was the third child of six. Coming from a farming background, he has lived a full and diverse life.

His education at a small local school, and then at three other institutions across Australia, set the stage for entering a life of work.

Learning a multitude of skills gave him competency in building with timber, fabricating steel, and mechanics. His experience with these skills made him a resource for others.

David loves to fix and invent new things and has created many items that could have been bought, but the excitement of making something new was a challenge too great to resist.

He enjoys all things aeronautical, as well as other means of travel. He is multi-skilled in the operation of heavy machines including agricultural, earthmoving, and transport. Before retirement he was a heavy transport operator for many years, travelling the interstates that stretch the length and breadth of the state.

Professionally, David is a competent public speaker, a certified Neuro Linguistic Programmer, and Hypnosis and Life Skills graduate. A deeply spiritual person, he constantly searches for answers to life's questions: where did we come from, what is our reason for being, and what kind of future is there for us as a species in the universe.

A lover of all things beautiful, especially in nature, David enjoys photography and recording life's special moments.

He has five children and fourteen grandchildren, all who are very much loved and important to him.

Kateřina Fišerová

Kateřina Fišerová is a transformative coach, mentor, writer, and founder of *The Listening World, Czechia Listens*, and *Happy School*.

She also serves on the board of the *Happy Czechia Foundation*, whose vision is to make the Czech Republic the happiest country in the world.

Guided by a deep love for life, Kateřina helps people rediscover their inner wisdom and wellbeing and fall in love with life again through simple yet profound conversations.

Together with friends, she co-founded the nonprofit *Understanding Human Mind* and co-leads a school for new coaches.

Fourteen years ago, Kateřina encountered the Three Principles, which completely transformed her experience of life. It was an honor for her to serve as a board member of the *Three Principles Global Community (3PGC)*, supporting the creation of new communities around the world. Today, Kateřina leads the Czech-speaking Three Principles community.

Before devoting her life to sharing this understanding, she led and later co-owned the email-marketing company *SmartEmailing* and founded several other businesses.

Following her heart, Kateřina now organizes *The Listening World Summit*, held annually in Prague and streamed freely to people around the world. She believes that "when we truly listen, the world changes."

Kateřina lives in the Czech countryside with her Czech-Slovak wolfdog, Honey, surrounded by forests, birdsong, and endless inspiration to listen: to life, to others, and to the quiet wisdom within.

Cory MacNeil

Cory A. MacNeil (DMin) lives in upstate New York near Saratoga Springs.

He has 25 plus years of customer service and ministry experience.

Cory is an avid outdoorsman and fisherman who loves spending time in the Adirondack Wilderness north of his home. Here, he finds solace in the ultimate place to recreate and show up for his family, friends, and clients as an energetic and positive Holistic Spiritual Life Coach.

Cory is an avid reader and greatly appreciates the work of Abraham Hicks, Sydney Banks, Byron Katie, Steve Hardison, and Steve Chandler, among others.

He also considers himself a late bloomer who is still nurturing and creating the relationships he has with his amazing wife, Nicola, and his three grown children. He is especially proud of the fact that his wife is from England and is still dumbfounded by her decision to move to the United States in 1997!

Cory embraces the philosophy of Super Coach Ankush Jain and aspires to raise the consciousness of the planet through coaching.

Coryamacneil@gmail.com
:www.facebook.com/CoryMacNeil

Diane Pierotti

Diane Pierotti was born on the lush, volcanic island of Réunion, a place where cultures, traditions, and legends intertwine. Of Chinese and French heritage, she grew up with a natural curiosity for both the seen and unseen worlds. Now based in Perth, Australia, with her Australian husband and their three boys, including a pair of lively twins, Diane's life is an ever-shifting dance between motherhood, creativity, and spiritual exploration.

From an early age, Diane was captivated by the mystical, as well as the way a story, dream, or symbol could open a doorway to deeper truths. This calling led her to become a tarot therapist and astrologer, guiding spiritually minded individuals back to the essence of who they are and why they are here. Diane's work blends insight, compassion, and a deep reverence for the soul's journey.

Whether through her sessions, or her writing, Diane's intention is to hold a lantern for others walking their own path of authenticity, reminding them that the greatest wisdom comes from embracing the truth of one's own heart.

Jojo Tonnaer

For as long as she can remember, Jojo has been able to converse with animals and the unseen world: spirits and beings from other realms. As a child, she often hid beneath the covers, fearful of the footsteps and guiding voices. Over time, Jojo realized that these early experiences were part of her intuitive gifts.

Raised in the south of the Netherlands near both the German and Belgian border, Jojo developed a love for languages and cultural connections. She perfected her languages through working in hospitality. This earned her an Erasmus scholarship to study Italian and French, leading to a career as a professional interpreter and international Show Producer for IBM Europe and Asia Pacific.

A turning point came when Jojo left the corporate world and moved to Florence to study jewelry design. Italy awakened her creative and intuitive expression. A serendipitous summer position in a crystal shop in Vieste opened the door to offering readings professionally.

After three years travelling through Europe and Africa, Jojo settled in Australia in 1999, where she continues to live and work. She has since trained in Nutrition, Kinesiology, Past Life Regression, Breathwork, and Body Psychotherapy (Somatic Therapy).

Since 2007, Jojo has guided clients as an Intuitive Healer, helping them reconnect with the deep wisdom of their body and embrace their vibrant, authentic selves. Her work is grounded in practical wisdom and her deep love for humanity. Jojo's skills have been honed through decades of experience, years of professional training, and a lifelong ability to read energy.

Jill Sawchuk

Jill Sawchuk is the mother of two beautiful humans and a full time yoga teacher. She has been practicing and sharing tools and teachings for health and wellness for over 25 years. She has taught thousands of people through countless classes and workshops internationally. Jill is curious and passionate about everything that helps us remember our true selves. After earning her bachelor's degree in education and having a near death experience early in her 20s, Jill's life has been guided by her heart, which has taken her to many places around the globe.

Jill lived in Mexico for 12 years and often traveled to India where she met many amazing teachers along the way. She is deeply influenced by the teachings of Vanda Scaravelli and Diane Long as well as the teachings of Vipassina as taught by S.N. Goenka. She hopes her legacy inspires more people to wake up to their divine nature and release all that holds them back from experiencing bliss, peace, and unity.

https://www.facebook.com/jill.sawchuk
www.yogajil.com

Alexis Godinez

There was a time when families living in Nicaragua were forced to flee their country in search of hope, freedom, and safety during the civil war. Through unimaginable adversity, they escaped bombs and bullets and eventually found refuge in Mexico City. There, Alicia Romero met a young man named Adrian Godínez. They fell in love and had a son (el nene) named Alexis Adrian Godínez.

Alexis came into this world a dreamer in search of truth. From a young age, he questioned everything, especially why humans needed money to survive when every other species lived in harmony with its environment. At just four years old, Alexis turned two lollipops into a large sum of money, not just for a child, but a large amount for any adult. From that moment on, he knew the art of creation was possible. That realization marked the beginning of his journey toward becoming self-made.

It wasn't until he was in his 30s that Alexis discovered the truth he had been searching for his entire life: the essence of God. Through every season, he has remained a man of faith—a man of God, never wavering.

Family has always been his greatest blessing. Alexis is a devoted son, a loving brother to David and Allison Godínez, and a brother to the world. He came into this life to love humanity and to shine a light so others could recognize their own. A lover of the good life, Alexis is deeply passionate about understanding spirituality and applying it to every aspect of life, including business. He believes that living by the laws of God opens the universe not for greed, but for balance, and allows one to live like the birds, in harmony with creation.

When Alexis was 29, the purest love entered his life—a love that would quietly change him forever.

That love was a dog named Rocky. Rocky became Alexis's safe space as he continued his journey in search of truth.

Kat Van Note

Kat Van Note was born on November 7, 1964, in Salt Lake City, Utah. A writer, researcher, and field resonance guide, her work weaves emotional precision, esoteric knowledge, and planetary patterning into grounded insight on the natural capabilities of humans wholly connected with nature.

She studied nutritional therapy and emotional release techniques, later developing her own method of unified field-sensing—long before such language entered the collective dialogue. While raising her four children in Idaho, Kat wrote quietly for years, often waking before dawn to listen to the field and chart human cycles.

In 2023, she completed 35 years of research, bringing forward decades of somatic tracking, symbolic pattern recognition, inner alignment, and pre-Western practices. Her writing merges science, mysticism, memory, and a return to ancient systems of nature—offering not answers, but orientation.

Kat travels internationally, participating in fireside conversations on awakening, alignment, and sensory awareness. She continues to live in Boise, Idaho, where she stewards a forested, community-rooted home and develops a body of work that includes *The Hidden Symbols of Astrology, Being Hum An,* a deep exploration of dimensional consciousness through the lens of the chakra, endocrine, and nervous systems, and *The Lumen Conduit,* a symbolic resonance map using fixed stars to align the human system with nature's creative potential.

Debbie Sears

Debbie Sears is a Nashville, Tennessee–based entrepreneur, writer, and mother who has built her life around truth, courage, and alignment. She grew up in Arkansas and later spent more than twenty years in the Los Angeles area—years that shaped her resilience, expanded her perspective, and helped shape the woman she is today.

Today, Debbie is deeply rooted in the vision of Spa Connections, the luxury wellness agency she acquired in 2018. Originally founded in 2006, the brand has evolved under her thoughtful guidance—grounded in integrity, excellence, and relationship-driven service. Her work reflects a belief that genuine care and connection never go out of style.

Debbie's world is deeply shaped by her love of music and her passion for exploring new places, two forces that keep her curious, open, and connected to the world around her. Most of all, she is moved by her four children—Sydney, Gabryella, Isabella, and Niko, who remind her daily what strength, devotion, and authenticity truly mean.

Now grounded in Nashville, Debbie steps into this chapter with clarity, purpose, and freedom. Her contribution to *The Art of Authenticity* reflects a woman who has learned to rise, rebuild, and return to herself—on her own terms.

Connect with Debbie:
Instagram: @debbiesears_
Facebook: debbie.lynn.sears

Darla Anne

Darla Anne's work as a clinical hypnotherapist is rooted in her own path toward authenticity, shaped by layered family dynamics and a lifelong search for inner alignment. Her grandfather, Leo Irby, was a renowned 1950s magician and escape artist known for slipping free from dramatic physical restraints. While his skills focused on breaking free from what externally confined him, Darla's professional path led her to help people release the inner bindings of limiting beliefs, self-doubt, and emotional noise, guiding clients out of inherited patterns and old stories that no longer serve them.

With over a decade devoted to this field, she graduated with honors from the Hypnosis Motivation Institute, earning both the Director's Award and the Academic Achievement Award. Darla is certified by the American Hypnosis Association and is currently completing her Advanced Occupational Studies degree in Mind Body Psychology. Her practice continues to deepen through teamwork and collaboration with a clinical psychologist, grounded in mentorship and a trauma-informed approach.

The heart of Darla's practice centers on the core premise that meaningful change begins in the subconscious. She helps clients shift internal responses, regulate the nervous system, and reshape beliefs that keep them feeling small or stuck. Her toolkit includes hypnotherapy, EFT Tapping, somatic techniques, advanced imagery, and integrative modalities offered in a compassionate, judgment-free space.

Darla's inspiration comes from walking alongside clients as they move through their journey to authenticity, guided by the kind of magic found not in escape, but in becoming who we were meant to be.

Connect with Darla on Facebook: Facebook.com/DarlaAnneCht

Emily Reid

Emily Reid is an Australian writer, poet, and humanitarian protection specialist with almost twenty years of experience across North Africa, the Middle East, and Asia. Her professional background spans cross-border migration, human trafficking, and humanitarian emergencies, working with the UN, governments, and non-profit organizations. Emily is passionate about supporting writers, especially refugee and displaced poets, to share their stories in ways that create hope, impact, and change.

She is the founder of Writers Rising, a not-for-profit platform that publishes and supports refugee and displaced poets, an initiative which won the People's Prize with RMIT Activator. Emily curated and edited Rohingya Dreams (2019), the first international anthology of Rohingya refugee poetry. The anthology was used as an advocacy tool that brought Rohingya poets to Geneva to raise awareness of ongoing forced returns to Myanmar. Her creative work spans fiction, nonfiction, and poetry, and is often informed by long-term professional experience in displacement and crisis contexts.

Emily is also a creative coach and breathwork instructor with Rebel Writers. She supports writers experiencing creative blocks, burnout, or difficulty sustaining a writing practice, combining practical writing tools, breathwork, and process-focused creative guidance.

Her creative publications include the spoken word album *Spark* (2024), an essay in the PEN International Journal, a poem in the London Writers' Salon Writing in Community anthology (2022), and a short story in a collected fiction volume. She is currently developing Poets on the Frontlines, a poetry and narrative project centered on writers in conflict and migration settings. Emily's forthcoming books include *The Last Dare*, *The Wild Writers*, and *Dancing with Shadows: How to Create in Times of Disaster.*

Instagram: https://www.instagram.com/emilyrebelwriters/
LinkedIn: https://www.linkedin.com/in/emily-reid/

Fiona Marie Williams

A woman who turned her ache into art and now helps others remember the truth they came here to live.

Fiona Marie is an Intuitive Medicine Woman, Transformational Mentor, Speaker, Somatic Healer, and truth-teller.

She supports both men and women in their return to their original essence, emotional clarity, and embodied power—where love becomes sacred, boundaries become clear, and authenticity becomes a way of life.

Through deep energetic transmissions, somatic practices, and transformational mentoring, Fiona guides others to remember who they were before they ever had to perform for love.

Connect with Fiona at fionamarie.org or on Instagram *@fionamarie.anahata*

Jason Bart

Jason Bart has been working with men and couples for over a decade. Facilitating workshops in Australia and around the world, he has developed a unique and natural way of inviting the powerful presence of Self to shine. His work involves encouraging individuals to look beyond the story, to see what is keeping their inner flame from shining bright, and allowing the Wisdom of our Authenticity radiate all that we do.

Freedom is a state of mind, and a state of being. It helps to define our boundaries, and what we are willing to accept in our lives.

If you are looking to dive deeper into your own truth, Jason could be the person to help you find it. With a gentle heart and strong will, he will guide you to your potential through the various stages of life, and the different songs that play out in our world.

"Peace comes when your actions reflect your authenticity."

— Unknown

AFTERWORD

I hope you enjoyed the heartfelt stories, wisdom, and vulnerability shared in this book. Storytelling is the oldest form of communication, and I hope you feel inspired to take a step toward living a fulfilling life. Feel free to contact any of the authors in this book or the other books in this series.

The proceeds of this book will be used for social giving at Jewel Children's Home in Northeast Bali.

Other books in the series are...

Your Inner Knowing : A Journey of Riches, Book Forty-Three
https://www.amazon.com/dp/B0GFL6PWMQ

Whispers of the Heart: A Journey of Riches, Book Forty-Two
https://www.amazon.com/dp/B0DPKBQNKF

Living into Self-Esteem: A Journey of Riches, Book Forty-One
https://www.amazon.com/dp/B0FGXQD289

Building Self-Confidence: A Journey of Riches, Book Forty
https://www.amazon.com/dp/B0F5PWWHPG

Unlock Your Hidden Potential: A Journey of Riches, Book Thirty-Nine
https://www.amazon.com/dp/B0DXVKT6KH

Follow Your Soul's Calling: A Journey of Riches, Book Thirty-Eight
https://www.amazon.com/dp/B0DQJYLBHY

The Power of Self-Discovery: A Journey of Riches, Book Thirty-Seven
https://www.amazon.com/dp/B0D4K35JFP

Elevating Your Life: A Journey of Riches, Book Thirty-Six
https://www.amazon.com/dp/B0CZWRJ94Y

Living the Paradigm of Kindness: A Journey of Riches, Book Thirty-Five
https://www.amazon.com/dp/B0CSXF1FBV

Creating Resilience: A Journey of Riches, Book Thirty-Four
https://www.amazon.com/dp/B0CNVRDY38

Discover Your Purpose: A Journey of Riches, Book Thirty-Three
https://www.amazon.com/dp/B0CFDLWTCB

Live Your Passion: A Journey of Riches, Book Thirty-Two
https://www.amazon.com/Live-Your-Passion-Stories-Fulfilling-ebook/dp/B0C5QXMNRQ

Master Your Mindset: A Journey of Riches, Book Thirty-One
https://mybook.to/MasterYourMindset

Transform Your Wounds into Wisdom: A Journey of Riches, Book Thirty
https://www.amazon.com/dp/ B0BKTJ377N

Motivate Your Life: A Journey of Riches, Book Twenty-Nine
https://www.amazon.com/dp/B0BCXMF11P

Awaken to Your Inner Truth: A Journey of Riches, Book Twenty-Eight
https://www.amazon.com/dp/B09YLYMQ4H?geniuslink=true

The Power of Inspiration: A Journey of Riches, Book Twenty-Seven
http://mybook.to/ThePowerofInspiration

Messages from The Heart: A Journey of Riches, Book Twenty-Six
http://mybook.to/MessagesOfHeart

Abundant Living: A Journey of Riches, Book Twenty-Five
https://www.amazon.com/dp/B0963N6B2C

The Way of the Leader: A Journey of Riches, Book Twenty-Four
https://www.amazon.com/dp/1925919285

The Attitude of Gratitude: *A Journey of Riches*, Book Twenty-Three
https://www.amazon.com/dp/1925919269

Facing Your Fears: *A Journey of Riches*, Book Twenty-Two
https://www.amazon.com/dp/1925919218

Returning to Love: *A Journey of Riches*, Book Twenty-One
https://www.amazon.com/dp/B08C54M2RB

Develop Inner Strength: *A Journey of Riches*, Book Twenty
https://www.amazon.com/dp/1925919153

Building your Dreams: A Journey of Riches, Book Nineteen
https://www.amazon.com/dp/B081KZCN5R

Liberate your Struggles: A Journey of Riches, Book Eighteen
https://www.amazon.com/dp/1925919099

In Search of Happiness: A Journey of Riches, Book Seventeen
https://www.amazon.com/dp/B07R8HMP3K

Tapping into Courage: A Journey of Riches, Book Sixteen
https://www.amazon.com/dp/B07NDCY1KY

The Power Healing: A Journey of Riches, Book Fifteen
https://www.amazon.com/dp/B07LGRJQ2S

The Way of the Entrepreneur: A Journey of Riches, Book Fourteen
https://www.amazon.com/dp/B07KNHYR8V

Discovering Love and Gratitude: A Journey of Riches, Book
Thirteen
https://www.amazon.com/dp/B07H23Q6D1

Transformational Change: A Journey of Riches, Book Twelve
https://www.amazon.com/dp/B07FYHMQRS

Finding Inspiration: A Journey of Riches, Book Eleven
https://www.amazon.com/dp/B07F1LS1ZW

Building your Life from Rock Bottom: A Journey of Riches, Book
Ten
https://www.amazon.com/dp/B07CZK155Z

Transformation Calling: A Journey of Riches, Book Nine
https://www.amazon.com/dp/B07BWQY9FB

Letting Go and Embracing the New: A Journey of Riches, Book
Eight
https://www.amazon.com/dp/B079ZKT2C2

Making Empowering Choices: A Journey of Riches, Book Seven
https://www.amazon.com/Making-Empowering-Choices-Journey-Riches-ebook/dp/B078JXMK5V

The Benefit of Challenge: A Journey of Riches, Book Six
https://www.amazon.com/dp/B0778S2VBD

Personal Changes: A Journey of Riches, Book Five
https://www.amazon.com/dp/B075WCQM4N

Dealing with Changes in Life: A Journey of Riches, Book Four
https://www.amazon.com/dp/B0716RDKK7

Making Changes: A Journey of Riches, Book Three
https://www.amazon.com/dp/B01MYWNI5A

The Gift in Challenge: A Journey of Riches, Book Two
https://www.amazon.com/dp/B01GBEML4G

From Darkness into the Light: A Journey of Riches, Book One
https://www.amazon.com/dp/B018QMPHJW

Thank you to all the authors who have shared aspects of their lives in hopes of inspiring others to live a bigger, fuller version of themselves.

I want to share a beautiful quote from Jim Rohn: "You can't complain and feel grateful at the same time." At any given moment, we can either feel like a victim of life or be connected and grateful for it. I hope this book helps you feel grateful and inspires you to pursue your dreams.

For more information about contributing to the series, visit our website: http://ajourneyofriches.com/. Furthermore, if you enjoyed

Afterword

reading this book, we would appreciate your review on Amazon to help get our message out to even more readers.